BLACK

AND

CATHOLIC

THE CHALLENGE AND GIFT
OF BLACK FOLK

CONTRIBUTIONS OF
AFRICAN AMERICAN EXPERIENCE
AND THOUGHT
TO CATHOLIC THEOLOGY

JAMIE T. PHELPS, O.P.
EDITOR

MARQUETTE
UNIVERSITY

PRESS

Marquette Studies in Theology
No. 5

Andrew Tallon, Series Editor

Library of Congress Cataloging-in-Publication Data

Black and Catholic : the challenge and gift of black folk :
contributions of African American experience and thought to
Catholic theology / Jamie T. Phelps, editor.
   p. cm. — (Marquette studies in theology ; #5)
   Includes bibliographical references and index.
   ISBN 0-87462-629-3 (pbk.)
   1. Afro-American Catholics--Religious life. 2. Catholic Church—
United States—Doctrines. 3. Afro-Americans--Religion. 4. United
States—Church history. 5. Christianity and culture—United States.
I. Phelps, Jamie T. (Jamie Therese), 1941- . II. Series.
BX1407.N4B56 1997
282'.73'08996073—dc21   97-45376

Marquette University Press
MILWAUKEE

The Association of Jesuit University Presses

Contents

Appendix 1
Foundations for Catholic Theology in an African American Perspective: The Bibliographic Essay

Appendix 2
The Sources of Theology: African-American Catholic Experience in the United States

Acknowledgement

I am most grateful to each contributor for the energy and time spent to bring this work to completion. Special words of thanks must be given to those whose collaboration in producing this completed volume was indispensable: Dr. Andrew Tallon, the Marquette University Press Director and Editor; the Marquette University Press staff and graphic artists; and my esteemed colleagues, Dr. M. Shawn Copeland and Dr. Patrick Carey.

About the cover and symbols:

These symbols and their interpretation were taken from a chart entitled "Meaning of Symbols in Adonkra Cloth, researched, written, and designed by Dr. KwakuOfori-Ansa, Associate Professor of African Art History, College of Fine Arts, Howard University, Washington, D.C.

GYE NYAME ("Except God")
Symbol of the Omnipotence of God

Proverb: "This Great panorama of creation dates back to time immemorial; no one lives who saw its beginning and no one will live to see its end, except God."

SANKOFA ("Go back to fetch")
Symbol of the wisdom in learning from the past in building the future

Proverb: "It is not a taboo to go back and retrieve if you forget."

ANANSE NTONAN ("The spider's web")
Symbol of wisdom, craftiness, creativity, and complexities of life

Folk tales and poems of Ananse the spider abound both on the continent of Africa and in the African dispora.

The color red was chosen in consistency with its traditional liturgical use as a symbol of the Holy Spirit and suffering. As such it symbolizes the blood and life of suffering which Black people endure in the United States and throughout the world because of their continued racial, gender, and class oppression. The power of the Holy Spirit has allowed them to survive, thrive, and overcome human obstacles to a full life.

Asanta symbols are traditionally used by Ansante fabric weavers for cloth woven for spiritual leaders and used in sacred ceremonies and rituals. Our three symbols suggest that the omnipotent creator God has given African American people the wisdom to go back and retrieve the truth of their human equality and dignity as recorded in the history, song, and proverbs of Africans and African Americans. The retrieval of these truths makes it possible for us to learn from the past in order to build the future. Historically, African American thought and creativity empowered by the omnipotent God has enabled us to build communities and organizations to protect and nurture black life despite the negative social, political, and economic forces which militate against our lives in our complex journey to overcome our marginalization and devaluation as African peoples. We must continue in that journey until all humanity no longer suffers humanly constructed structural and interpersoanl injustice.—Jamie T. Phelps, O.P.

Preface

Patrick W. Carey

This book is the first of its kind. I know of no other book in which African-American scholars jointly address issues related to the African-American Catholic experience. I know of no other book in which Catholic theology and theological education is discussed in light of the African-American experience. I know of no other book in which African-American Catholic scholars have published their collective concerns about the state of Catholic higher education.

Some might think that the African-American Catholic is a minority within a minority in the United States. There is much truth in that generalization but, like most generalizations, it gives a false impression—at least from the demographic perspective. Recent surveys and opinion polls indicate that there are about 2.5 million African-American Catholics (about 3 percent of the total Catholic population and about 9 percent of the total African-American population). That number seems insignificant until one realizes that there are more African-American Catholics than there are members of a good many American Protestant denominations. There are more African-American Catholics, for example, than there are Adventists, Disciples of Christ, Quakers, Jehovah's Witnesses, Mennonites, African Methodist Episcopal Zion Church members, and African Methodist Episcopal Church members.

African-American Catholics, too, have been a significant part of the history of American Catholicism and the American religious tradition, although until most recently they have received little attention in the major histories. At the end of the eighteenth century, twenty percent of American Catholics, as John Carroll indicated in a report to Rome, were African-Americans.[1] That percentage decreased significantly in the course of the nineteenth century with the influx of European immigrants. Nonetheless, the story of African-American Catholics is a significant part of the American Catholic tradition. It was a history of slavery and oppression, but also one of African-American Catholic initiative in founding religious orders and raising a lay consciousness in the nineteenth century, and in constructing self-help programs and in calling for reforms in the Catholic Church, Catholic education for African-Americans, and social justice in the twentieth century. In fact, the present book fits within the long history of African-American Catholic attempts (e.g., the nineteenth century African-American Catholic Congresses and the twentieth century Federation of Colored Catholics) to address the issue of education for African-American Catholics. This book is part of an already established tradition of criticism and creative reform— this time within Catholic higher education.

Contemporary African-American Catholics, recent scientific surveys demonstrate, have a higher educational success rate than the overall American average regardless of race. In 1990, the City University of New York conducted a national survey of religious identification that revealed the overwhelming success rate of African-American Catholics in completing high school and college. That survey showed, moreover, that 40 percent of African-American Catholics are more likely to graduate from college than other African-Americans. In the 40 to 59 year-old age group, 26 percent of African-American Catholics, 25 percent of white Catholics, and 24 percent of all whites and 15 percent of all African-Americans are college graduates.[2]

From the late nineteenth century onwards leaders in the African-American Catholic community have pushed for education for their children and for Catholic educational institutions to take a leading role in providing that education. Endemic racism and lack of financial resources prevented an adequate response to these calls for massive institutional support for primary and then secondary education for African American Catholics. Only gradually did the Catholic educational institutions at all levels integrate African-Americans into their institutions.

This book is a beneficiary of those past achievements in education and a call for a new kind of reform in Catholic higher education, one that pays particular attention to the inclusion and integration of the African-American experience in Catholic theology and in the entire curriculum—particularly in the hermeneutical enterprises in theology, ethics, scripture, and history.

There are many ethnic and racial components in the Catholic tradition. This book is a challenge to that tradition not just to include courses in the curriculum on the African-American experience (we already have a proliferation of unconnected courses in the curriculum), but to transform the entire curriculum in such a way that the unity of the educational experience will be enhanced by the diversity of the traditions that make up that unity.

Notes

[1]Thomas O'Brien Hanley, ed., *The John Carroll Papers,* 3 vols. (Notre Dame, IN: University of Notre Dame Press, 1976), 1:179.

[2]Seymour P. Lachman and Barry A. Kosmin, "Black Catholics Get Ahead," *New York Times* 14 September 1991.

Introduction:
Theology from an African American Catholic Perspective

Jamie T. Phelps, O.P.

In his recent work entitled "The Opening of the American Mind," Lawrence W. Levine notes that

> The United States has always been a multicultural, multiethnic, multiracial society, but in our own time these truths—and their implications for higher education—have become increasingly difficult to ignore. As the university becomes more open to and representative of the diverse peoples, experiences, traditions, and cultures that comprise America, its impulse to find explanations for those parts of our history and our culture we have ignored grows proportionately. It has to enable our students to comprehend the nature of the society they're part of, the history of groups and traditions they will interact with, the meaning of ideas and experiences they will inevitably encounter.[1]

The recognition of the plurality of cultures and histories of the world community in general and in the United States in particular has posed a challenge to higher education whether that education is taking place in the university or graduate level seminaries. The challenge affects every aspect and level of education. Racial and cultural inclusivity in the composition of the faculty, curricula, and teaching methods are considered imperative so students can be prepared for the social plurality they will encounter after they leave their formal studies and begin to minister in today's church and world.

In U.S. Catholic seminaries and university related schools of theology and/or divinity, the recognition of the increased number of Hispanics who make up the U.S. Catholic reality has led to the practice of requiring all seminarians to become literate in the Spanish language and to engage in some study of Hispanic culture. To date a similar mandate has not been forthcoming relative to the study of the history, culture and theological perspectives of African Americans, Asian Americans, and Native Americans.

Accrediting bodies, academic deans, curriculum committees and faculty members have many questions about whose experience and what texts should be included in their academic canons. To assist in the debate at the Catholic Theological Union as it relates to the experience of African Americans, I proposed a combined academic and pastoral conference to bring the predominantly European American faculty into dialogue with African American Catholic scholars, the Black Catholic community, and its ministers. The conference was co-sponsored by the Catholic Theological Union at Chicago and three offices of the Archdiocese of Chicago: the African American Desk of Ethnic Ministries Office (EMO), the Center for the Development of Ministry (CDM), and the Office for Religious Education (ORE). Sheila Adams (EMO), Rosalie Henebry-Keane (CDM), and Joyce Gille (ORE), representatives from these offices, served as the major co-planners. All the faculty members of the Association of Chicago Theological Schools (ACTS) were invited to participate.

Two of the six goals identified for the conference related specifically to the academic component:

1) "To engage the faculty of the Catholic Theological Union and Association of Chicago Theological Schools in a discussion of the content, methods, and sources necessary to integrate the questions arising from Black American experience and pastoral context into their regular curriculum and course work."

2) "To assist the administration and faculty of predominantly white theological institutions in 'integrating' black faculty, students, and issues into the mainstream of their curriculum and institutions."

The following essays and responses represent the experience, research, and argument of African American scholars and their European American colleagues engaged in a dialogue to explore the question of including the experience and questions arising from the social location of the African Americans within the curricula of theological schools and seminaries. Limited by time constraints the discussion only included the disciplines of history, scripture, ethics, and systematics.

My introductory essay, "African American Catholics: The Struggles, Contributions, and Gifts of a Marginalized Community" provides a thumbnail sketch of African American Catholic history with special emphasis on the goals of the nineteenth and twentieth century Black Catholic Movements and their thoughts regarding the mission of the U.S. Catholic Church to the African American Community. In this context, the essay provides an historical overview of the history of Black Roman Catholics in their quest both for recognition of their full humanity and for active participation in developing action plans for strengthening the African American presence in the Roman Catholic church as well as for building up, expanding, and transforming our nation and our church.

In the second essay, "Reclaiming the Spirit: On Teaching Church History: Why Can't They Be More Like Us?," Dr. Cyprian Davis, O.S.B., discusses the problem of including the history of Blacks and Black Catholics within the main curriculum of historical studies. The discipline of history as including church history has shifted in the last thirty years from the exclusive chronicling of the history of the monarchs, conquerors, and famous and infamous persons of the day, to a history of ordinary peoples. What has emerged is a method of doing history "from below." This shift in approach has provided opportunity for those peoples whose history has been relegated to the margins to emerge from those margins. Davis concludes by outlining six goals for the teaching of church history.

Dr. Zielinski concurs with Dr. Davis's assertion of the importance of history in theological studies. He further notes that one result of employing the method "from below" is the discovery of "poignant examples of fidelity to the universal vision of the church" on the part of African American Catholics. He suggests that the "historical example of faith-filled witnesses in the African American Catholic community are rich resources for contemporary theological reflection." Finally, Dr. Zielinski applauds Davis's six goals for teaching history as clarifying and challenging, and suggests a seventh one: The study of history should provide a medium for teaching students the "art of interpretation" which will assist them in reading the signs of the times.

In his essay, "Reading Texts Through Worlds, Worlds Through Texts," which focuses on biblical interpretation, Dr. Vincent Wimbush analyzes how African American experiences and worldviews have served as the interpretive lens through which the Bible has been appropriated as a source of "psychic spiritual power and inspiration for learning and affirmation." He argues that the notion of biblical interpretation as discovering the objective, true meaning of the "texts" through historical critical scholarship or ecclesiastical pronouncements is misguided. According to Wimbush, biblical interpretation is the science and art which involves the complex process of the mutual interpretation of "worlds" and "texts." The social location and worldview of the contemporary interpreter influences his or her interpretation of the social location and worldview of the biblical world. In a similar manner, contemporary interpretive texts not only reveal the meaning of the texts as they functioned in their original context but also produce new texts that reveal the meaning of the Bible for the diverse social-cultural realities of the worlds of contemporary interpreters.

Dr. Bergant basically concurs with Dr. Wimbush's argument and reminds us that all interpretations are "both limited and biased." Culturally specific works such as those of Dr. Wimbush must be studied by all students to sharpen their "historical accuracy and intellectual integrity." She notes that the method of mutually critiquing historical and textual criticism employed in his biblical essay appropriately involves, as Dr. Wimbush suggests, a critique of the history of interpretation itself. Bergant suggest that these methodological considerations are the most valuable insights and contributions Black scriptural scholars are making to the field of biblical interpretation.

Dr. Bryan Massingale argues effectively that "our conception, articulation, and realization of the good is affected to no small degree by the color-consciousness of North American (European) theology and ethics." Asserting that "Americans cannot pursue the ethical quest or moral issues with integrity and responsibility without being attentive to the reality of racism," he challenges his Catholic colleagues in the field of ethics by demonstrating their glaring omission of the treatment of that topic in the major theological organs of their discipline. This critique is followed by a constructive review and interpretation of the characteristics of African American religious ethics as demonstrated in the work of his African American Protestant colleagues: (1) "an empathetic insistence upon and unreserved commitment to the principle of the freedom and equality of all persons under God"; (2) "a passionate concern for justice"; and (3) "an ethic of hope." He concludes his essay with a clear delineation of the division of the ethical question/task which black and white ethicists must share, and the normative vision of African American ethicists.

Dr. Wadell's response acknowledges that Dr. Massingale accurately cites omission of the topic of racism from the work of most American Catholic ethicists, and suggest that the major reason for this omission lies in the "prevailing methodology of Roman Catholics ethics today." While agreeing with Dr. Massingale's designation of the central question of Christian ethics as "what manner of living is congruent with belief in the God of Jesus Christ?" he explains three shifts in Catholic ethics which have deflected Catholic ethicists from focusing on this central question: (1) the collapse of the distinction between being human and being Christian; (2) the desire to forge a universal morality which leads "to [a] general, abstract, and unhistorical understanding of humanity"; (3) and the absence of hospitality in the dominant methodology, i.e., the lack of concern about the experience of African Americans. He concludes by underscoring three characteristics of African American religious ethics as both challenges and contributions to Catholic ethicists.

In the final comprehensive essay on systematic theology, Dr. Copeland adapts the method of Bernard Lonergan for her exposition. Discussing the task of systematic theologians, she raises the question of available foundations for a Catholic theology in an African American context, then traces the African American sources for such a theology by discussing the emergence of Black religious experience as it was transformed from African traditional religions on the African continent to the "attitudes, convictions, gestures, symbols, rituals, beliefs, and structures" of Black Religion in the United States. This experience found its first theological expression in the spirituals. She concludes her essay with an outline of ten marks which should characterize an "African American Catholic Theology" and the cultural authenticity and theoretical truthfulness of the claims of the theological propositions of African American Catholic Theology as represented in the work of those who engage in the work of Catholic theology as it relates to African American experience. Her bibliographic essay in the appendix includes key resources for those wanting to explore the terrain of Black Theology further.

Readers should find this collection of essays stimulating, provocative, and rich with critical insight about the complexity of African American experience, and find even richer the terrain it provides for theological research and pastoral ministry. Each contributor has identified key issues to be considered in any curriculum that wishes to address the particular concerns impacting the lives of African Americans in general and African American Catholics in particular. Each essay speaks of the desire on the part of African Americans and African American Catholics to experience the recognition of their essential human equality and the gifts they bear. Each essay encourages us to "be attentive!" to the reality of African Americans whose life-centered struggles and contributions to the church and nation are usually marginalized and invisible in theological curricula. Each essay identifies themes that lie at the heart of African American existence in the United States and weaves passion for justice throughout the essays: the quest for human freedom, the desire for racial unity and universal inclusion as counter to the pervasive reality of racist exclusion, the reality of a God-given hope. Collectively, these essays affirm a methodology "from below" which begins the theological inquiry from the concrete daily and historical experiences of African Americans. If Christian theology is to be an articulation of truth predicated on the vision of the reign of God proclaimed by Jesus the Christ, it must also be a theology that transforms our intellectual understanding of ourselves, our God, and others; it must endow us with a sense of empathetic compassion; it must change our patterns of relationships from the habits of exclusion to patterns of inclusion. Acceptance of the Roman Catholic doctrine[2] of God's universal love and justice must lead us to respect and embrace all peoples.

Notes

[1]Lawrence W. Levine, *The Opening of the American Mind: Canons, Culture and History* (Boston: Beacon Press, 1996). This text provides a revealing and insightful historical analysis of the role culture and history have played in the development of academic canons.

[2]This doctrine is not the exclusive property of Roman Catholicism; many Christian churches and other religious traditions subscribe to similar teachings.

African American Catholics: The Struggles, Contributions, and Gifts of a Marginalized Community

Jamie T. Phelps, O.P., Ph.D.
Catholic Theological Union: Chicago, Illinois

Introduction

As a professor of theology in the context of a graduate school of ministry, it is my goal to help my students grow as critical thinkers and Christian disciples as they prepare to exercise their roles as ordained and lay ministers within the Catholic Church. Such ministry must be grounded in knowledge of the theological, biblical, and magisterial traditions which are the articulations of ever-changing expressions of our limited rational and faith-rooted understandings of the mysteries of God, humanity, and creation. In their search for personal authenticity, life-giving truth, and effective ministerial methods, students preparing for ministry engage in critical reflection on their own and others' experience, and they examine the moral behavior of individuals and diverse cultural groups in the light of the Gospel and the teachings of the church. In the pages that follow, I will provide a general interpretive overview of the social and historical dilemma of marginalization and devaluation that Black Catholics confront within the context of the dominate culture's worldview of our nation and of the Roman Catholic Church in the United States. The essay is primarily a synopsis of the presence and contributions of Black Catholics as they struggle to share their gifts within the church despite their experiences of marginalization within the church and despite their invisibility within the nation.

The Problematic

The inclusion of African Americans as full and equal citizens within the American journey of the United States has been fraught with rejection, ambiguity, and struggle. This struggle within society in general is paralleled by the struggle of African American Catholics to be recognized as fully human children of God, disciples of Jesus Christ, and full and equal members of the Catholic Church in the United States.

In 1903, W.E.B. Dubois, an African American graduate of Fisk and Harvard Universities and a student and friend of Max Weber at the University of Berlin, described the existential dilemma of African Americans in an essay entitled "Of Our Spiritual Strivings." Struggling to discover the meaning of his own life and the life of others who are oppressed and viewed as less valuable and human than members of the dominant culture, Dubois poignantly articulated the psycho-social Angst:

> ... It is a peculiar sensation, this double consciousness, this sense of always looking at one's self through the eyes of others, of measuring one's soul by the tape of a world that looks on in amused contempt and pity. One ever feels his twoness—an American, a Negro; two souls, two thoughts, two unreconciled strivings; two warring ideals in one dark body, whose dogged strength alone keeps it from being torn asunder.

He continues in the language appropriate to his early twentieth century context:

> The history of the American Negro is the history of strife—this longing to attain self-conscious manhood, to merge his double self into a better and truer self. In this merging he wishes neither of the older selves to be lost. He would not Africanize America, for America has too much to teach the world and Africa. He would not bleach his Negro soul in a flood of white Americanism, for he knows that Negro blood has a message for the world. He simply wishes to make it possible to be both Negro and American, without being cursed and spit upon by his fellows, without having doors of opportunity closed roughly in his face. This, then, is the end of his striving: to be a co-worker in the kingdom of culture, to escape both death and isolation, to husband and use his best powers and his latent genius. These powers of body and mind have in the past been strangely wasted, dispersed, or forgotten.[1]

U.S. Black Catholics of the late twentieth century can paraphrase these words of Dubois. Black Catholics simply wish to make it possible to be Black, Catholic, and American without being cursed and spit upon, devalued and marginalized by other Blacks, Catholics, or Americans. We would like to live free of the experience of having the doors of churches, universities, workplaces, corporate boardrooms, and residential communities closed in our faces. Blacks have been and continue to be formally and informally ostracized from or marginalized within social and/or ecclesial institutions. The 1989 National Research Council's report, "Common Destiny: Blacks and American Society," identifies three factors that perpetuate the marginalization of Black Americans: "Three...barriers to full opportunity for Black Americans are residential segregation, continuance of diffuse and often indirect discrimination, and exclusion from social networks essential for full access to economic and educational opportunities."[2] In a similar vein, the U.S. Catholic Bishops' 1979 Pastoral, "Brothers and Sisters to Us," cited the continued presence of racism manifested clearly by the reality that "in the very places in which Blacks, Hispanics, Native Americans, and Asians are numerous, the Church's officials and representatives, both clerical and lay, are predominantly white."[3]

The failure to see or acknowledge black presence and contributions to the church and the society is a by-product of the social sin of racism. Institutionalized racism so blinds the minds, eyes, and hearts of those infected with its pernicious sense of white supremacist ideology that few perceive the patterns of racial exclusion and segregation that infect the dynamics of institutions. These racist dynamics are viewed as normal and ordinary by most members of both the dominant and oppressed cultures.[4] The history of the dominant culture's exclusion of African Americans from full participation within its social institutions and the history of the contributions of African Americans to church and society, despite their social exclusion, are often ignored, denied, or deliberately omitted.[5]

Most often the presence of Black Roman Catholics is ignored, compacted, or footnoted within major historical and statistical research about either Roman Catholics or African Americans in the United States. The complex history of the Catholic Church's relation to African Americans is seldom explored. Several historical works on the Catholic Church in the United States by John Tracy Ellis, Jim Hennessey, and Jay Dolan do acknowledge the African American presence, but few acknowledge this African American presence as an integral part of the Catholic mainstream.[6] Although historian John

Gillard wrote at least three full books on the "Negro" in the Catholic Church in 1929, 1935, and 1941,[7] the publication of Cyprian Davis's *The History of Black Catholics in The United States* in 1990 was historic because of its perspective, quality, and subject matter, as well as its publication and marketing by a major publisher.[8] In a similar vein, major African American religious histories by E. Franklin Frazier, Gayraud Wilmore, and C. Eric Lincoln generally focus on the historically Black denominations while giving minimal or negative interpretations to the presence and contributions of Black members and congregations within the Roman Catholic Church or other denominations in the United States, which are predominantly white. The work of religious historian Albert J. Raboteau is a notable exception to this rule.[9]

The assumption of the statistical insignificance of Black Catholics in the U.S. Catholic population is seldom challenged or analyzed. Most Roman Catholic dioceses and parishes do not have or use a regular systematic, standardized, and objective method of gathering ethnic-cultural statistics. Yet statistics are often used to legitimate closing Catholic institutions in predominantly black geographic areas. One reason given for the closing of Catholic schools and churches in the inner city is the fact that most of the population in the community and schools are non-Catholic; yet in the past these schools and churches have been the base for the church's evangelizing efforts among African Americans. The church's mission of evangelizing, social justice, and charity has never been restricted to Catholics alone. Viewing itself as a universal sacrament of salvation, the Church has traditionally extended herself to all persons, regardless of their national, cultural, or religious affiliation. Anti-black racism has played a role in the mission of the Catholic Church in the United States different from its role in other nations. Culturally sensitive evangelizing strategies are needed today to invite African Americans to consider Roman Catholicism as a Christian way of life that can assist them in their quest to be authentic human beings in the journey to full communion with God and others. Many traditions of doctrine and social justice in the church provide strong theological rationales for the quests for human freedom, dignity, and justice; these quests are foundational to African American social ethics. Despite their invisibility, marginalization, and devaluation, Black and/or African American Roman Catholics number somewhere between 2,300,000

(03.9%) and 3 million of an estimated total of 59 million Roman Catholics in the United States.[10] Juxtaposing this number with the 3.5 million Catholics of Ireland, as reported in a 1992 television report, and the estimated 131,535,540 millions of Roman Catholics on the continent of Africa, reveals the provincialism and relativity of the term "statistically insignificant" and counters the assumption that African and African American cultures are fundamentally incompatible with Catholic culture. The 1990 work of C. Eric Lincoln and Lawrence H. Mamiya, *The Black Church in the African American Experience,* reported that the African American Catholic population in 1985 was approximately 2 million, according to a 1989 Gallup Survey reported in the July 15, 1989 New York Times. The authors noted that "Since 1985, Black Roman Catholics have been among the fastest growing religious groups, largely due to the influx of Haitians and other Black people from the Caribbean region. Upwardly mobile African Americans have been attracted to parochial school education as a result of the problems of urban public schools systems."[11]

U.S. Social-Cultural History

African American Catholics experience a double invisibility, marginalizaion, and devaluation. In the Black world we are marginalized because of our religious identity as Catholics; and in the Catholic world we are marginalized because of our racial and cultural identity as African Americans. The situation is further complicated when the economic and gender locations of some African American Catholics are taken into consideration. Poor, black, African American Catholic women experience an intensification of marginalization and devaluation.

The social marginalization of Black Catholics in the United States is shared with all Blacks and other oppressed peoples within our nation. This marginalizaion is rooted in the historical development of the United States. Paradoxically, those seeking the recognition of their full human dignity through the acquisition of social and religious freedom have sometimes concomitantly denied the recognition of the full human dignity and acquisition of social and religious freedom of others. Africans and Native Americans were either enslaved, segregated, placed on reservations, or murdered. They were neither acknowledged as fully human nor as children of God.

Social marginalizaion, with its concomitant invisibility and devaluation, is perpetuated when historians and others refer to the United States as a "nation of immigrants." This description ignores the existence of non-immigrant populations. Most Native Americans and Africans did not "immigrate" to this continent during the colonial period. The colonial and ecclesial expansion of Spain, France, and England, which began in the fifteenth century with explorers and colonial pioneers, continued with successive fluctuating waves of immigrants until the first half of the twentieth century. European refugees immigrated to the United States to seek political, religious, and economic freedom. The immigrant perspective of U.S. history, though partially true, glosses over the negative impact of colonization and immigration upon the lives of the Native peoples and Africans in the early foundation of our nation.

Different circumstances conditioned the origins and presence of the ancestors of present-day Native Americans, African Americans, Asian Americans, and Mexicans Americans within our nations history. The United States is the homeland of Native Americans,[12] believed to have migrated in various waves from Asia between 19,000 to 10,000 years ago.[13] African Americans were "marketed" on the west coast of Africa after being captured or sold into slavery by African collaborators. These slaves were legally identified as "chattel" or "talking animals," and were used as a labor force under a brutal system of slavery.[14] This slave-labor force was later augmented by the importation of "foreign workers," e.g., by the importation of Chinese "temporary" workers who were "employed" for the development of the railroad system in the United States. Mexican Americans became a part of the nation as boundaries shifted with the acquisition of some of the Northern sections of Mexico from Central America.

The origins of racial marginalization and its concomitant "double consciousness" are rooted in the destruction and pain inflicted upon the ancestors of Native Americans and upon their culture, as well as in the slavery and deaths of the ancestors of African Americans who died during the "middle passage." In both cases, the personhood and culture of Native Americans and Africans were ignored and denied. The isolation of Native Americans on reservations and their genocide during the period of Western expansion was justified by denying their full humanity, by denying their land rights, and by fear of their retaliatory violence. The genocide of Africans during the slave trade of the Middle Passage, and their brutal treatment as slaves, were, similarly, justified by denying their full humanity, by denying them any human rights, and the fear of their retaliatory violence.

A more inclusive and accurate designation of the population of the United States would be that the United States is a nation comprising descendants of native peoples, European immigrants, enslaved Africans, and continuous waves of economic and political refugees and immigrants from Europe, Asia, Africa, Latin America, and the Caribbean. At the dawn of the twenty-first century we are a culturally diverse nation. Succinctly, the United States is a microscopic cultural mosaic of the cultural diversity that characterizes the global world.

U.S. Religious History

The religious history of Christian expansion parallels that of the nation's social history. The social-cultural complexity of our Colonial History (1492-1780) provided the context for the first chapter of the mission history of the United States. Columbus and subsequent explorers and missionaries from Spain, Portugal, France, and England came to these shores not only as emissaries of their Queens and Kings but as "instruments of God" with a divine mission and gospel mandate to "go out all over the world and preach the gospel to all creation." Conquest and conversion, as church historian Jay Dolan documents, were expansionist partners.[15] The underside of the colonial enterprise castes shadows on the history of missionary expansion: the conquest of Native Americans, the enslavement of Africans, and the segregation of both on reservations and plantations respectively. Christian churches not only were silent regarding the immorality of these processes but often aided and abetted the conquest by provided a religious legitimation for such actions. Notions of cultural, racial, intellectual, and moral superiority, coupled with a theology of "manifest destiny," grounded both colonial and missionary expansion.[16]

Both Indians and Africans were victims of overt, direct social violence arising from the conflict of expansion and nation building.[17] The brutalization and marginalization which denied the full humanity of our ancestors continues covertly within the social and ecclesial institutions whose members treat the masses of Native Americans, Blacks, and selected groups of Hispanic and Asian Americans as intellectually, morally, and spiritually inferior. This negative treatment manifests the reality of the social sin of racism which divides the human community.[18]

Two million plus people should not be regarded as insignificant or expendable from the pages of history or the ministerial focus of the broader Catholic community. A review of most histories of American Catholicism in the United States—there are some notable exceptions—reveals, however, that this is precisely what has happened in the past and continues to happen in the present.[19] Ethnic-racial divisions and their concomitant ethnic-racial hierarchies of human value based on false notions of race, skin color, and culture have led to an obsession with race, to the point that race silently undergirds most interactions in the social and ecclesial communities in the U.S.[20] The racial-ethnic divide is so pervasive that the history of many racial-ethnic groups within the United States is generally unknown. The history of African Americans, Native Americans, Asian Americans, and Hispanic Americans is neither known nor systematically and organically included in the history curricula. The integral relationship of the history of these culturally diverse groups to the history of European Americans is seldom reflected accurately. The primary sources for history: oral narratives, archives, institutional records, etc., manifest the integral relationships of colonial explorers and settlers, native Indians, African slaves, and black and white indentured servants during the colonial period, but, until most recently, U.S. history focused primarily on the experience and perspectives of the colonizers. The history of the victims of U.S. colonial expansion has been relegated to margins or to collected anecdotes in volumes of general U.S. history. Black and Indian history is found in separate volumes which often are not part of the required curricula of study.

As noted above, the phenomenon of the marginalization of specific cultural groups on the pages of history is also manifest in the history of Roman Catholics in the United States. A constructive development toward the correction of the omission of the history of Roman Catholics of African American descent from the pages of U.S. Roman Catholic history has been the publication of several separate volumes of history which document the experience of Black Catholics in the United States among these are: Marilyn Nickels, *Black Catholic Protest and the Federated Colored Catholics 1917-1933,* Cyprian Davis *The History of Black Catholics in the United States,* and Stephen Och *Desegregating the Altar.*[21] In addition some recent dissertations have retrieved some significant aspects of the history, presence, and contributions of Black Catholics during the nineteenth and twentieth centuries. My own dissertation "The Mission Ecclesiology of John R. Slattery: A Study of an African American Mission of the Catholic Church in the Nineteenth Century," which includes a great deal of historical documentation, was completed at The Catholic University in 1989. Thaddeus Posey's dissertation, "An Unwanted Commitment : The Spirituality of the Early Oblates Sisters of Providence," completed at Saint Louis University in 1993, and Cecilia Moore's dissertation, "A Brilliant Possibility: The Cardinal Gibbons Institute: 1924-1934," completed at the University of Virginia in 1996, all contribute to the efforts to recover the complex history of Black Catholics based on primary sources.[22] The works of Davis, Posey, and Moore provide an account of African and African American presence and contributions to the Catholic Church in the United States, while the other works detail the dynamics and struggles of the Catholic Church in the United States as it sought to respond to the needs, presence, and participation of black people in the U.S. Church and society. All the works provide historical interpretation of the struggles and involvement of Black Catholics, religious and lay, in the mission of the Catholic Church among African Americans during the nineteenth and twentieth century.

Blacks in the Early Church

Beginning in Africa, as most contemporary histories of African Americans do, Davis's historical account locates the black presence in the bible by noting the references in the Song of Songs to the queen of Sheba (Songs 1:5) and in Origen, the great Alexandrian church father of the third century, who comments on this verse. Sheba represented the universal church, i.e., all the races beyond the Hebrew world of the Old Testament. Origen noted the black wife of Moses and the Kushite, Ebed-Melech, who saved the life of Jeremiah. Davis noted that the Kush is the biblical name for Nubia a Black African nation which by the eight century before Christ had become the dominant power. When the Nubian King Kashta died in 750 B.C. his Son, Piankhi, began the XXVth Dynasty, the reign of the Black Pharaohs and warriors spoken about in Isaiah 18ff. The New Testament also documents the presence of Black Ethiopians in the person of the "Ethiopian Eunuch" baptized by the Deacon Philip

(Acts 8:26-40). All these events occurred before the conversions of Paul and the Roman Centurion Cornelius, who was converted by Peter. The Ethiopian Eunuch is the first documented Black African to enter the Christian faith. Davis also documents the African presence among the early fathers and popes of the Church. Origen, Augustine, Tertullian, St. Victor, St, Militiades, and St. Gelasius were all Africans.[23] St. Victor, the first Latin speaking bishop who was pope from 189 to 199, introduced Latin as the standard language of the Church. St. Militiades was pope during Constantine's rise to Roman imperial and ecclesial power. St. Gelasius, noted most for his contributions to the splendor of the Roman liturgies, was pope from March 1, 492 to November 21, 496.[24]

U.S. Black Catholics in the Nineteenth Century

Although the presence of Black Catholics in the colonies had been documented as early as 1536,[25] in the latter half of the nineteenth century the presence of emancipated Catholic black slaves was acknowledged, and the question of expanding the Catholic Mission among this population became an item on the common agenda of the Bishops of the Church in the United States during the second and third plenary councils of Baltimore.[26] The discussion of the evangelization of slaves before and after emancipation and the fate of those free persons of color and slaves who had already been baptized Catholic during this period were recorded in the archives of Catholic history as problematic. First the church found herself confronted with "the problem of emancipation!" Many Bishops and religious orders of men and women held slaves, and the emancipation of a large working force would prove competitive to those "immigrant Catholics" who themselves were on the margins of the great American expansionist program. The church maintained a "neutral" silence regarding the question of slavery, regarding it as a social rather than religious question. The leading moral theologian of that time, Francis Patrick Kenrick, asserted that "slavery was not a contradiction of the natural law which viewed all human beings as equals whose basic rights as persons must be protected"[27] Second, the bishops were confronted with the "problem" of the post-emancipation education of blacks. Most Catholic schools of this period did not accept blacks within their student body, and those industrial schools which did were generally segregated. Third, the bishops were confronted with the "problem" of admitting Black men to priesthood and women to religious life. Most, though not all, church members and leadership viewed the Negro as morally and intellectually inferior and therefore unsuited for priesthood or vowed religious life. This attitude was confounded even more by the fact that civil laws forbidding Blacks and Whites to live under the same roof proved an acceptable rational to perpetuate the exclusion of Blacks from such ministerial roles within the church. This practice was first discussed collectively by the U.S. hierarchy in a closed session of the Second Plenary Council of Baltimore in 1866. Fourth, there was the "problem" of establishing churches that would allow Blacks to worship in Catholic Churches. Once baptized, Blacks faced the general practice of the Catholic Churches, which was to arrange separate worship services for its Black members or to relegate their presence to the back pews or galleries.[28]

Nineteenth and Twentieth Century White U.S. Catholic Initiatives

Not all White Catholics interpreted the presence of Blacks as a problem. Though most members of the nineteenth-century U.S. Catholic Church were oblivious to African roots and of African contributions to the Roman Catholic Church, the African presence in the early Church and the expansion of the Church in Africa in the nineteenth century captured the imagination and creative thinking of John R. Slattery, an Irish Catholic Mill Hill Missionary from New York, who sought to initiate the Mill Hill/Josephite mission of the Catholic Church among the newly emancipated slaves in the latter quarter of the nineteenth century.[29] Slattery initiated the first successful effort to establish a process for admitting Black men to priestly formation and to priesthood as members of integrated religious congregations. In 1888, two years after Rome ordained Augustus Tolton as the first recognized African-American priest and sent him to the missions of the United States, Slattery opened St. Joseph's Seminary in Baltimore to train Black and White men for ordained ministry among African Americans. In 1889 he established Epiphany Apostolic College.[30]

In 1890, Katherine Drexel, a member of the prestigious and wealthy Philadelphia banking family, founded the Sisters of the Blessed Sacrament for Indians and Colored People. The primary mission of this congregation of women was the evangelization of Native and African Americans. Not only did Katherine Drexel provide personnel for evangelization and education of Blacks and Indians, but she and her sister, Louise Drexel Morell, both used their inheritance to extend extensive financial support to various projects and initiatives directed toward the benefit of Native and African Americans. Both supported the National Association for the Advancement of Colored People's anti-lynching campaign. Katherine funded the building of Catholic schools and churches to serve Indians and Blacks and supplied the Sisters of the Blessed Sacrament as faculty for these endeavors. Her most notable educational foundation was Xavier University of Louisiana in New Orleans. This University was and still is the only Black Catholic institution of higher learning in the United States.[31] Louise Drexel Morell was a major financial contributor to the seminary, schools, and parishes and other initiatives of John R. Slattery which were directed toward the education and development of African Americans.[32]

In 1909, Conrad Rebesher, pastor of the Most Pure Heart of Mary parish in Mobile, Alabama, initiated the Knights of St. Peter Claver in response to the need of a fraternity for Black Catholic men. It was organized as a benevolent association to supply insurance for the welfare of its members' families at the time of the member's death. Members were also "mobilized for charitable work and for assistance in programs on the diocesan level."[33] Rebesher invited several other Josephites and three black laymen to join him in the founding of the Knights.[34] The organization gradually expanded its membership to other African Americans by establishing the "junior knights" (for male children and teens) in 1917, the Ladies Auxiliary of Peter Claver (for Adult females) in 1922, and the "junior daughters "for female children and teens) in 1930.[35]

Nineteenth Century U.S. Black Catholic Initiatives

Supported by a select few White Catholic bishops, clergy, religious, and laity, Black Catholics initiated an organized ministry to blacks. Prior to the Second Plenary Council of Baltimore, two orders of religious women were founded through the initiative of Black women, Elizabeth Lange, a Haitian born Cuban, and Henriette DeLisle. Elizabeth Lange, who founded the Oblate Sisters of Providence in 1829, began her ministry as a laywoman providing education to the children of Black Cuban refugees in Baltimore. Henriette Delisle, a free woman of color, had worked with the slaves and poor.[36] Upon the

Foundation of the Sisters of the Holy Family in 1842, she expanded the ministry to care for the sick and orphans, and to provide education for girls from the families of free Blacks in New Orleans.[37]

The Negro Catholic Congresses (1889-1895)

Neither the foundation of the black religious orders of women nor the opening of seminaries which would train Black men, nor even the establishment of schools for Negro children, was accomplished without conflict within and beyond the U.S. Catholic Church. A Black Catholic journalist, Daniel Rudd, perceived the Catholic Church as a friend to Blacks which offered Black people material and spiritual refuge superior to all the inducements of other organizations combined.[38] At Rudd's initiative, supported by other Black Catholic laymen and selected white clergy, five Lay Catholic Congresses were conducted to address the concerns and interests of Blacks.[39] During the First Congress (January 1, 1889) the delegates acknowledged the continued obstruction of the "sacred rights of justice and humanity" of Black people. The members pledged to aid in the establishment of schools for all levels of education and to encourage the works of Whites, both Catholic and non-Catholic, who were establishing industrial schools, orphanages, and hospitals to work for "the regeneration of our people."[40]

The Second Congress (1890) focused on the need for secondary schools for boys and "for full religious education of Catholics, regardless of color or race."[41] Trade unions were asked to admit Blacks with full participation and privilege, and employers were encouragd to employ young black men and women as clerks. The general public was asked to care for orphans and to abolish the slave trade. "The delegates pledged to work to obtain men and women who would enter the brotherhood and sisterhood to advance the interest of their race in the faith."[42]

The Third Congress (1892) continued the emphasis on the need for Catholic education for black children, though there was debate on whether these schools (and Catholic churches) should be segregated or integrated, given the climate of the times. A commission was appointed to form a committee to investigate the "practice of discrimination against Black children in Catholic Schools"[43] and the Congress also established itself as a permanent organization.

The Fourth Congress (1893) was held in conjunction with the World Columbian Catholic Congress in Chicago. The issue of racial discrimination within the Church was clearly identified in the context of the debate about integrated and segregated Churches. The Fifth Congress (1894) further explored the question of racial discrimination within the Church. It was noted that although racial discrimination was not sanctioned by law in the diocese, the practice of individual parishes needed to be denounced. Blacks did not want special treatment but did aspire to being treated as "earnest, honest, members of the Church."[44] The practice of caste distinction within the Church was deplored by the Black Catholic laymen.[45]

The speeches of the Black Catholic laymen who initiated and committed themselves to the Congress movement identified several theological themes as foundational to their endeavor. Their theological anthropology underscored the essential equality of human beings because of "fatherhood of God and the brotherhood of man."[46] "The first great necessity of any man [*sic*] or nation is to know God his creator, to fully understand his relations and obligations to him [God] and his own eternal destination."[47] The mission of the church as moral teacher, liberator, and defender of the oppressed was understood as a continuance of God's concern for the oppressed as witnessed in the Old Testament. They trusted that the Bishops, as officials of the institutional church, would join and support them in their efforts to transform the social condition of Blacks.[48] One speaker clearly identified their action as inspired and empowered by the grace of the Holy Spirit.[49]

Congress speakers anticipated the communion-centered ecclesiology of the Second Vatican Council, its understanding of the integral relationship of the social and spiritual conditions of people, and the mission of the church as a universal sacrament of salvation. The foundation and participation of nineteenth-century Black Catholics in the parishes, schools, and religious orders, and the inauguration of the Negro Catholic Congresses, were gifts of unconditional love for Christ and for the U.S. Catholic Church. Black Catholics and their supportive clergy and religious confronted the institutional racism which characterized the practice of their White Catholic sisters and brothers in the faith. Confronting the underside of the U.S. Catholic Church led the nineteenth-century ancestors of African American

Catholics to realize what "Lumen Gentium," the dogmatic constitution on the church, promulgated at the Second Vatican Council.

> ...the Church in Christ is in the nature of sacrament—a sign and instrument, that is, of communion with God and the unity of all men...
> ...the church [of Christ] constituted and organized as a society in the present world, subsists in the Catholic Church...[this church] clasping sinners to her bosom at once holy and always in need of purification, [must follow] constantly the path of penance and renewal. ...
> Christ lifted up from the earth has drawn all men [and women] to himself. Rising from the dead, he sent his life-giving Spirit upon his disciples and through him set up the Body, which is the Church as the universal sacrament of salvation.[50]

Black Catholics demanded and continue to demand that the Church examine and cease its racial discriminatory practices. Their demands underscore the Church's teachings on the essential spiritual and historical communion of all men and women, and points to the Catholic Church's role as universal sacrament of the unconditional love of Jesus the Christ. Such demands reveal Black Catholics' consciousness and fidelity to the church's teaching in these areas. They understand that life in the Spirit of the risen Christ compels one toward communion with their non-Black brothers and sisters as an integral aspect of their communion within church and society.

Twentieth-Century U.S. Black Catholic Initiatives

Thomas Wyatt Turner, professor of biology and member of St. Augustine's Catholic Church in Washington, D.C., inherited the spirit and legacy of his Black Catholic ancestors. Turner initiated the Federated Colored Catholics at a simple gathering in his home in 1917. Initially identified as the "Committee Against the Extension of Race Prejudice in the Church," the members wrote letters to the hierarchy about the "discriminatory practices within the church, the lack of proper educational facilities for black children, and the urgent need of a black priesthood."[51] Intended by Turner to further the agenda of the N.A.A.C.P., the committee was renamed the Committee for the Advancement of Colored Catholics within the Catholic Church in 1919. The Federation's 1925 constitution states several purposes for the organization: 1) to bring about a closer union and better feeling among all Catholic Negroes; 2) to advance the cause of Catholic education throughout the Negro population; and 3) to seek to raise the general Church status of the Negro and to stimulate colored Catholics to a larger participation in racial and civic affairs.[52]

Under Turner's leadership, eight annual conventions were held between 1925 and 1932. Some of the key issues discussed included education, employment and the participation of Blacks within the organizations and structures of the Church. Fr. John LaFarge and William Morgan Markoe join the movement to assist the black lay men and women but shifted the aims of the lay movement. Under their influence the movement became more ecclesially focused as "Catholic Action." The concern for the betterment of Black Catholics was transformed into concern for "interracial justice" focused on the transformation of white Catholic attitudes.[53] The re-direction of the original focus of the Federated Colored Catholics through the well-intentioned though subversive presence of William Markoe and John LaFarge caused heated conflicts which led to the death of the organization. The National Catholic Interracial Conference on Interracial Justice emerged from the ashes of the Federated Colored Catholics.[54]

The Contemporary Black Catholic Movement (1968-Present)

It was not until April 16, 1968, that Black-Catholic initiative would re-assert itself nationally when Father Herman Porter, a black priest of the diocese of Rockford, Illinois, founded the National Black Catholic Clergy Caucus (NBCCC). Father Porter was the vice president of the Catholic Clergy Conference on the Interracial Apostolate (CCCIA) and he convened the NBCCC as a "meeting within the meeting" of the CCCIA when it met in Detroit. The first meeting of the NBCCC, attended by Black Catholic priests and one Black Catholic woman religious, declared that "The Catholic Church in the United States, primarily a white racist institution, has addressed itself primarily to white society and is definitely part of that society."[55] This statement further advocated:

1. That there be black priests in the decision-making position on the diocesan levels, and above all in the black community.
2. That a more effective utilization of black priest be made...that black be priests given a choice of assignment on the basis of inclination and talent.

3. That where no black priests belong to the diocese, efforts be made to get them in...

4. That special efforts be made to recruit black men for priesthood...

5. That dioceses provide centers for the training of white priests intending to serve in black communities.

6. That within the framework of the United States Catholic Conference, a black department be set up to deal with the Church's role in the struggle of black people for freedom

7. That in all these areas black religious be utilized as much as possible.

8. That black men, married as well as single, be ordained permanent deacons to aid in this work of the Church.

9. That each diocese allocate substantial funds to be used in establishing and supporting permanent programs for black leadership in training."[56]

The National Black Sisters Conference was founded in August, 1968, by the former Sister Martin DePorres Grey, R.S.M., who had been present at the first NBCCC meeting. The NBSC proposed to "work unceasingly for the liberation of black people. Expression of individual and institutional racism found in our society and Church are declared by us to be categorically evil and inimical to the freedom of all men, and particularly destructive to black people in America." The NBSC identified seven major purposes:

1. the development of the individual black sisters themselves and the deepening of the spirituality, unity, and solidarity of black religious women by annual conferences of seven to ten days, black retreats, publication of a black sisters' newsletter; publication of the proceedings from the annual conferences and retreats, and a panel to explain in depth to black religious communities the purpose and organization of the National Black Sister's Conference.

2. to study, speak, and act on conditions and issues in the social, educational, economic, and religious milieu in the United States which involve moral and Christian principles.

3. to importune our society, especially our church and religious congregations, to respond with Christian enthusiasm to the need for eradicating the powerlessness, the poverty, and the distorted self-image of victimized black people by responsibly encouraging white people to address themselves to the roots of racism in their own social, professional, and spiritual milieu, through encounter groups with white religious congregations, and research and action on racism in social, educational, professional, and spiritual milieus, particularly in the Catholic environment.

4. to help promote a positive self-image among ourselves and our black people through the knowledge of and appreciation for the beauty of our rich historical and cultural heritage by development of a clearing house for black resources and consultative services, and development of black curriculum workshops.

5. to give impetus to boldly innovative forms of community action and to participate in existing programs in the civic communities of which we are members, by organizing seminars on understanding the dynamics and implementation of community action and control.

6. to initiate, organize, and participate in programs through which we can educate ourselves and our black people, thereby encouraging the utilization of those resources which are useful to black people.

7. and to develop and utilize the full potential represented by the National Black Sisters Conference through the effective participation of the National Office of Black Catholic, and through the initiation and endorsement of all activities and programs which can support and enhance the growth of black leadership within the church and in our religious communities by a symposium on black liturgical designs, understanding and utilizing spiritual and gospel music, black theology, black sister's formation, and the black apostolate.[57]

Members of these first two Black Catholic Organizations in turn supported the founding and development of several National Black Catholic organizations by some of its participating members: the National Office of Black Catholics in 1970 by Br. Joseph M. Davis, S.M.,[58] the National Black Seminarians Conference in 1970, the National Black Catholic Lay Caucus around 1975, and the National Association of Black Catholic Administrators in 1978.[59] The meetings of these groups independently and in joint conferences became the fertile ground which nurtured the convening of the first Black Catholic Theological Symposium (BCTS) in 1978 by Thaddeus Posey, O.F.M. Cap.; the writing of the USCC pastoral "Brothers and Sisters to Us: Racism in our Day" (developed by the National Catholic Conference of Bishop under the guidance of Bishop Joseph Francis, S.V.D.); and the founding of the Institute for Black Catholic Studies at Xavier University in 1982 as a first fruit of the Black Catholic Theological Symposium.

The original BCTS met only twice. In 1982, Thaddeus Posey, its founder, shifted his primary attention to the foundation and directorship of the Institute for Black Catholic Studies. In 1991, after a long hiatus, Jamie Phelps, re-established the Symposium and in consultation with the participants transformed it into a national professional society for African American Catholic scholars. Membership is open to African American Catholics holding doctoral degrees in theology or disciplines related to theology, e.g., philosophy, religious education, psychology, literature, history, sociology, etc. The Symposium was re-established:

1. to foster among Black Catholics an ethical community of scholarly dialogue characterized by
    a. commitment to the fundamental humanity of all persons;
    b. regard for the plurality of cultural, ethnic backgrounds and religious experience among Black peoples;
    c. the development of a theology which is authentically Black and truly Catholic.
2. to publish reports, the Symposium's discussions, and research of Symposium membership;
3. to encourage the teaching and discussion of Black Catholic religious and cultural experiences through and within the theology and/or religious studies curriculum of colleges, universities, and seminaries;
4. to encourage the identification and development of Black Catholic scholars in the fields of Theology, Liturgy, Ethics, Canon Law, Church History, Biblical Studies, etc.;
5. to enable the identification and development of theoretically grounded practitioners in the fields of pastoral ministry and religious education; and
6. to encourage theologically and theoretically grounded ministry and program development responsive to the needs of Black Catholics within the Church and society.[60]

A major expansion of the movement occurred with the convening of the sixth and seventh National Black Catholic Congresses in 1987 and 1992 by the African American Bishops in the United States. The 1987 conference attended by approximately 1500 delegates representing 107 dioceses, which represented the two million Black Catholics of the United States.[61] The 1987 plan comprised three major sections: 1) the Black and Catholic identity of Black Catholics as mediated by the local parishes and dioceses, 2) the necessity of developing Black Catholic leadership to participate in decision making, evangelization, and parish development, and 3) the "outreach" ministries of the Catholic church, i.e., Catholic schools, social and economic issues, parish participation in community organizations, and community development.

The contemporary Black Catholic Movement (1968–) has spawned institutions, publications, and liturgical reform within the U.S. Catholic Church. These reforms were initiated by Black Catholics and ratified by the official church. Through its efforts the National Catholic Conference of Bishops were inspired to participate in the naming of thirteen Black Catholic Bishops and have given informal approval to Black Catholic liturgical innovation. The bishops have also supported and recognized the institutions and organizations initiated by Black Catholics as the gifts of Black Catholics to the church and society.

Having been inspired and empowered by the same Spirit who guided their Black Catholic predecessor, representatives of the National Black Catholic Organizations planned the Seventh National Black Congress which convened June 9–11, 1992 in New Orleans. The 1992 Congress comprised 2700 voting delegates and some 91 bishops. Entitled "The African American Family," the focus was on two broad categories: public policies and pastoral recommendations. Issues of a national family policy, Medicaid, universal health care, welfare-reform, the job training partnership act of 1982, the job opportunities and basic skills training program, the multi-cultural curriculum, and scholarships for higher education were addressed under the umbrella of the first category. The issues of African American family life, marriage as a sign and sacrament, the laity and family life, children and youth, religious education and catechesis, catholic schools, the family and African American ministries, diocesan structures which address family life, pastoral ministries to families, African American Catholics and public policy, and evangelization and family life were addressed under the second category. Both congresses continue to broaden the scope of the social and religious issues that are key to nurturing and sustaining the human dignity and life of Black people within our nation and church, issues which had been identified by the black lay leaders who participated in the first five African American Catholic Congresses in the nineteenth century.

Conclusion

In the preceding pages I have presented a general overview of the historical conditions and dynamics which have served to marginalize and devalue the presence and contributions of African Americans within our nation and within the Catholic Church. Secondly, I have provided a thumbnail sketch of some of the history of contributions of white and black Catholics to the mission of the church among African Americans. The sketch was not exhaustive nor was it intended to be. In conclusion I would like to note some observations about the past and future contributions of Black Catholics to the Catholic mission among African Americans.

1. In the past, African American Catholics, gifted by the presence and power of the Holy Spirit and inspired by the mission of Jesus Christ and the church, built schools, churches and other institutions in which the lives of Black American children would be nourished mentally, spiritually, and morally.

2. Today, we are challenged with the necessity of assuming responsibility within our church and society to continue this legacy of institutional building. If we don't use God's gifts to us to heal the brokenness of our community, no one else can or will.

3. As lay Black and/or African American Catholics we have the obligation and ability to initiate those programs needed within our parish and communities which will continue the mission of Jesus Christ in much the same way as those who have gone before us.

4. Black Catholics must initiate and collaborate with our pastors and all those who seek honestly to assist us in responding to God's gift of grace within us.

5. Effective ministry in the African American community requires a good heart as well as a good mind. The complexity of our lives and our tasks requires that those wishing to commit themselves to ministry in the church must deepen their knowledge of both the Roman Catholic Christian traditions and the experience of the peoples and cultures among whom they wish to minister. This seems to require on-going theological education as well as the study of various aspects of psychology, sociology, history and economics as these impact on the life and well being of African peoples.

6. If Blacks do not respond to their call to participate in the mission of the church both within the church and the society—there will be no future for Blacks in either our church or our nation. If we reclaim the gift of the Spirit, of prayer, study, and hard work, all things are possible. We have been called as Christians to assist in the transformation of both the Black community and the Catholic Church as we continue the ministry of Jesus Christ among the poor.

7. The power of the Spirit enables those who are oppressed by the church and other social institutions to continue to create, contribute and grow in communion with one another and God, despite their oppression. The gift of Black Folk is a gift given to us by the Creator,

sustained by the compassion of the Redeemer and vivified by the power of the Holy Spirit. It is essentially the gift of compassionate healing and transformative reconciliation.

Notes

[1]This essay was first published in 1903 and is reprinted as W.E.B. Du Bois, *The Souls of Black Folk* (New York: Bantam Books, 1989) 3.

[2]National Research Council, *A Common Destiny: Black and American Society* (Washington, D.C.: National Academy Press, 1989) 9.

[3]National Conference of Catholic Bishops, *Brothers and Sisters To Us: U.S. Bishops' Pastoral on Racism in Our Day* (Washington, D.C.:United States Catholic Conference, 1979) 11.

[4]See James Boggs, *Racism and Class Struggle* (New York: Monthly Review Press, 1970) 147-48. "Racism is the systemized oppression of one race by another. In other words, the various forms of oppression within every sphere of social relations—economic exploitation, military subjugation, political subordination, cultural devaluation, psychological violation, sexual degradation, verbal abuse, etc. ... together make up a whole of interacting and developing processes which operate so normally and naturally and are so much a part of the existing institutions of the society that the individuals involved are barely conscious of their operation. As Fanon says, 'The racist in a culture of racism is therefore normal.'"

[5]Often when African Americans excel in the fields of their expertise their ethnic-cultural identity is overlooked or deemed insignificant by such statements as "I hardly noticed that they are black!" Such statements could suggest that blacks must overcome ethnic-cultural identity in order to excel. Unconsciously such a view seems to equate whiteness as an exclusive ontological condition for goodness and genetically determined success while blackness is an ontological manifestation of evil and genetically determined failure. Such attitudes belie the reality of the human potential of all persons—a potential which is only realized by nurturing and developing their minds, hearts, and skills by disciplined study and work.

[6]See John Tracy Ellis, *American Catholicism* (Chicago: University of Chicago Press, 1956). James Hennessy, *American Catholics* (New York: Oxford University Press, 1981). Jay Dolan, *The American Catholic Experience* (New York: Doubleday, 1985).

[7]John Gillard, *The Catholic Church and the American Negro* (Baltimore: Josephite Press, 1929). John Gillard, *The Negro American: A Mission Investigation* (Cincinnati: Catholic Student Crusade Mission, 1935). John Gillard, *Colored Catholics in the United States* (Baltimore: Josephite Press, 1941).

[8]Cyprian Davis, *The History of Black Catholics in the United States* (New York: Crossroad, 1990).

⁹See for example, the classic study of E. Franklin Frazier, *The Negro Church in America* (New York: Schocken Books, 1964). Gayraud Wilmore, *Black Religion and Black Radicalism: An Interpretation of the Religious History of Afro-American People* (New York; Orbis Books, 1983; 2d ed.). C. Eric Lincoln and Lawrence H. Mamiya, *The Black Church in the African American Experience* (Durham: Duke University Press, 1990). The thirty-one page bibliography in the Lincoln-Mamiya text, though lacking a single reference to Black Catholic history, is a valuable source for Protestant Black Church history and sociology. In the Introduction, the authors intentionally restricted their subject to the "seven major historic black denominations...[although they] recognized that there are predominantly black local churches in white denominations such as the United Methodist Church, the Episcopal Church, and the Roman Catholic Church..." The work of religious historian Albert J. Raboteau, a former Roman Catholic, is perhaps the most notable exception to this rule. His works *Slave Religion* (New York: Oxford University Press,1980) and *A Fire in The Bones: Reflections on African-American Religious History* (Boston: Beacon Press,1995) span the Catholic-Protestant divide.

¹⁰The 1993 U.S. Catholic Almanac and David Barrett, ed., *World Christian Encyclopedia* (New York: Oxford Press, 1982) 782-85. Some sources predict that the world-wide population of Roman Catholics who are African (Continental Africans) or of African descent (i.e., the African Diaspora I, and Africans who were enslaved or migrated to the Caribbean, the United States and Europe) will exceed 200,000,000 by the year 2000.

¹¹C. Eric Lincoln, *The Black Church*, 407.

¹²Carol Hampton, "A Heritage Denied," *Sojourners* 20 (1991): 11-13.

¹³Russell Thornton, *American Indian Holocaust and Survival* (Norman: University of Oklahoma Press, 1987) 10. See also Miguel Leon-Portilla, *Endangered Cultures* (Dallas: Southern Methodist University Press, 1990) for an anthropological and ethical discussion of cultural conquest and transformation.

¹⁴Kenneth M. Stampp, *The Peculiar Institution* (New York: Vintage Books, 1956).

¹⁵Jay Dolan, *The American Catholic Experience* (New York: Doubleday, 1985): 15-68.

¹⁶Bishop Griffin, "Reflections on Evangelization, Yesterday, Today and Tomorrow" *Origins* 21(1991): 58-66.

¹⁷Davis 1990, 286; Lester B. Scherer, *Slavery and the Churches in Early America: 1619-1819* (Grand Rapids: Eerdmans,1975). Stephen J. Ochs, *Desegregating the Altar* (Baton Rouge: Louisiana State University Press, 1990), 9-48. Jamie T. Phelps, "The Mission Ecclesiology of John R. Slattery: A Study of an African American Mission of the Catholic Church in the Nineteenth Century" (Ph.D. diss.,The Catholic University of America, 1989) 6-146.

¹⁸National Conference of Catholic Bishops (1979) 10.

[19]In recent years, due to the commitment of its editor, Christopher Kauffman and editorial board, the research of select few Catholic Historians and other scholars who focus on this topic is periodically published and discussed in the *U.S. Catholic Historian* published by the U.S. Catholic Historical Society. See Volume 6 Number 1 (1996); Volume 7 Numbers 2 and 3 (Spring/summer, 1988); Volume 12 Number 1 (Winter, 1994).

[20]See Andrew Hacker, *Two Nations: Black and White, Separate, Hostile and Unequal* (New York: Ballantine Books, 1995; 2d ed.), for an analysis of the negative impact of racial division in America upon all Americans.

[21]Marilyn Nickels, *Black Catholic Protest: and the Federated Colored Catholics, 1917-1933* (New York: Garland Publishing,1988). Davis 1990. Ochs 1990. As noted in note 19, more Catholic historians both black and white are participating in the retrieval and publication of the history of Black Catholics.

[22]Phelps 1989. Thaddeus J. Posey, O.F.M., Cap. "An Unwanted Commitment: The Spirituality of the Early Oblate Sisters of Providence." (Ph.D. diss., Saint Louis University, 1993); Cecilia Moore, "A Brilliant Possibility: The Cardinal Gibbon's Institute, 1924-1934," (Ph.D. diss., University of Virginia, 1996). These dissertations and are available through the University Microfilm International, Ann Arbor Michigan.

[23]See also Patrick Granfield, *The Papacy in Transition* (New York: Doubleday, 1980) 197.

[24]Davis 1990, 2-14.

[25]Davis 1990, 28.

[26]Phelps 1989, 101-21;145; 263-74.

[27]Phelps 1989, 71.

[28]Interestingly enough, many Black Catholics saw this ecclesial segregation as a contradiction of the church's teaching on the basic equality of human beings and many spoke against the practice; see Jamie T. Phelps, "John R.Slattery's Missionary Strategies" *U.S. Catholic Historian: The Black Catholic Community, 1880-1987,* 7 (1988): 205.

[29]Phelps 1989, 245.

[30]Phelps 1989,177-78.Davis 1990, 145-62. Ochs (1990) is the definitive historical research on Slattery's efforts in this area.

[31]Davis 1990, 112, 136, 254.

[32]See Josephite Archives correspondence between Lady Morrell and John R. Slattery.

[33]Davis 1990, 235-36.

[34]Davis 1990, 236.

[35]Davis 1990, 236.

[36]Davis, 1990, 99-105. Phelps 1989, 83-84. Posey (1993) focuses on the history and spirituality of the Oblates Sisters of Providence. A synopsis is published as "Praying in the Shadows: The Oblate Sisters of Providence, a Look at Nineteenth Century Black Catholic Spirituality" *U.S. Catholic Historian* 12 (1994): 11-30.

[37]Phelps 1989, 83-84; Davis 1990, 105-15. See also, Joseph H. Fichter, S.J., "The White Church and the Black Sisters," *U.S. Catholic Historian* 12 (1994): 31-48.

[38]Phelps 1989, 122.

[39]The primary source for information of the first three Catholic Congresses is a copy of the published proceedings. Daniel A. Rudd, ed., *Three Catholic Negro Congresses* (1883 ed.) reprinted as *Three Catholic Afro-American Catholic Congresses* (New York: Arno Press, 1978).

[40]Phelps 1989, 126.

[41]Phelps 1989, 129.

[42]Phelps 1989.

[43]Phelps 1989, 134.

[44]David Spalding, "The Negro Catholic Congresses 1889-1894," *The Catholic Historical Review* 55 (1969): 352.

[45]Phelps 1989, 121-44. Davis 1990, 164-94

[46]Rudd 1978, 24

[47]Rudd 1978, 97.

[48]Rudd 1978; Rudd's Speech 24-25;59. See Dr. Lofton's Speech, 95.

[49]Rudd 1978, 67.

[50]"Lumen Gentium," *Vatican Council II: The Conciliar and Post Conciliar Documents*, ed., Austin Flannery, O.P. (Northport, New York: Costello Publishing Company, 1986; study edition) 1,8, 48.

[51]Nickels 1988, 3.; "Thomas Wyatt Turner and the Federated Colored Catholics," *U.S. Catholic Historian* 7(1988): 215-32.

[52]Nickels 1988, 303.

[53]Nickels 1988, 286-314.Davis 1990, 217-29.

[54]See Martin A. Zielinski, "Working For Interracial Justice: The Catholic Interracial Council of New York, 1934-1964. *U.S. Catholic Historian* 7(1988): 233-60.

[55]Davis 1990, 258. The full text of the statement can be found in "A Statement of the Black Catholic Clergy Caucus," Black Theology: A Documentary History, Volume One: 1966-1979, eds. James H. Cone & Gayraud S. Wilmore (New York: Orbis Books, 1993): 230-32.

[56]Cone and Wilmore 1993, 230-31.

[57]Martin DePorres Grey, R.S.M, *Black Women As Part of the Answer* (Washington, D.C.: National Black Sisters Conference, 1971): 26-27. An earlier version of the commitments is outlined in "The Survival of Soul: National Black Sister's Conference Position Paper," *Black Survival: Past-Present-Future: Conference Papers of the Second National Black Sisters Conference* (NBSC) (August 6-16. 1969) (Washington D.C.: National Black Sisters' Conference, 1970): 155-59.

[58]Joseph M. Davis, S.M., and Cyprian Rowe, F.M.S., "The Development of the National Office for Black Catholics," *U.S. Catholic Historian* 7 (1988): 265-89.

[59]Carole V. Norris, "Offices of Black Catholic Ministry: Heralds of a New Era," *U.S. Catholic Historian* 7(1988): 291-96.

[60]Article I of the By-Laws of the Black Catholic Theological Society drafted and presented to the BCTS participants at their annual meeting in June of 1993 by Jamie T. Phelps, O.P. The amended version was passed at the 1993 annual meeting in San Antonio.

[61]Nickels 1988, vi. Phelps 1989, 355-59.

Reclaiming the Spirit:
On Teaching Church History:
Why Can't They Be More Like Us?

Cyprian Davis, O.S.B., D.Hist.Sc.
St. Meinrad School of Theology: St. Meinrad, Indiana

Jumièges was a Benedictine abbey founded in the ninth century in the northwest part of France, known as Normandy. Today only magnificent and imposing ruins remain of what was once the wealthiest abbey in Normandy. It was on a summer day that I went to see these ruins. I was working at the time on my doctorate in history, concentrating on medieval monastic history. I had a duty in piety and an obligation to scholarship to make the short trip from where I was staying to the site of this ancient abbey. The monks with whom I was staying drove me, but I had to shift for myself in coming back. I anticipated no problem. This was a time when the wearing of the religious habit by the hitchhiker guaranteed a lift. Sure enough, two French priests in their cassocks and berets picked me up in their small French car. There was space in the back but no seat. The conversation began. "Where was I from?" "The United States." "I suppose you have nothing like this in your country?" "This" meant, of course, the ruins of Jumièges. I readily agreed. No American abbey is as beautiful as Jumièges even in its ruined condition. The interrogation went on. "Where is your family from?" How do I answer that? "Your people? They had to come from somewhere." I said that they came from Africa. The response was quick and terse, like a whip: "They don't have anything at all like this down there."

The two French priests did not know that they had in their car an ardent Francophile, who when De Gaulle spoke, I listened; someone who loved everything French from the wines of Bordeaux and Camembert cheese to Edith Piaf and Fernandel. The words seared: "There is nothing like this down there." I was a guest, I was polite, and I did not want to walk. I said nothing. The trouble is I did not know what to say. It is not only that I have never acquired the French ability to devastate your neighbor with exquisitely chosen phrases that are so extremely polite that they become unmistakably rude, but I did not know how to disprove the statement. I learned then that the study of history is also a means for self-defense.

Today I would be able to say that unfortunately *Monsieur le Curé* is sadly mistaken, that there are some marvelous architectural wonders in most parts of Africa. I would mention that the Ethiopians—already Christians for 600 years before Rollo, the Viking, plunderer and first duke of Normandy, was baptized in 911—had constructed churches more fantastic and more beautiful even than Jumièges. I would tell him that the Ethiopians did not build the great churches of Lalibala, but that they excavated them, literally chiseled them out of the living rock after excavating the rock formation planted deep in the ground. I would tell him that these fantastic churches shaped like a Greek cross, carved out of the living rock beginning in the early thirteenth century, have sculpted windows, with the interior of the rock hollowed out for the nave and the aisles and the walls covered with frescoes.[1] I would tell him that there are some thirty or more rock-hewn churches like those of Lalibala all over Ethiopia but none like them in all of France. For the Ethiopians, I would tell him, "on this rock I will build my church" had another meaning: they hollowed out the rock and made it a church.

In a sense the Church and the rock have been our problem for a long time. What do you do with the rock? Make it into a wall? Split it apart and use the pieces to bombard the enemy? Build upon it or build within it? This morning I would like to talk about giving everybody a piece of the rock and letting them come together to build the church into a house; I want to talk about teaching Church history in a worldwide perspective. I shall have four headings and a conclusion: Perceptions and perspectives; Rethinking the context; Rewriting the goals; Truth and consequences; and a conclusion.

Perceptions and Perspectives

Over twenty years ago, Léopold Génicot, my major professor at the University of Louvain, wrote a long reflection on the need to enlarge our studies of Church History, to move from a history of structures and institutions to a history of members, from a history of the papacy and the episcopacy to a history of the faithful themselves, from a history of conciliar decrees to a history of those affected by the decrees. He called for a history of Catholicism, which was, as he said, "the incarnation of the Gospel message and how it was made known, how it was understood, and how it was lived." He then pointed out that the next step was to broaden the horizons from Catholicism to Christianity.[2]

For the last thirty years or so, a new kind of history has been promoted by secular historians and, as my professor was an example, it has been taken up by Church historians. It began with French historians who belonged to what was known as the "*Annales*" School, who, from about 1930, sought to wean historians away from studying only national, political, or military history. They stated that not only popes and kings made history but ordinary people as well. The idea was that everybody had a history and an historical study could be made everywhere. For that reason it was important to study not only the battles during The Hundred Years' War but also the sewage facilities in 14th-century towns at the time of the Bubonic Plague.[3]

This new history has many facets and also has its detractors, but it has affected every student of history in the past two decades. In its broadest aspect, it is called "history from below." For Church historians this means that we cannot know the Church if we do not know ordinary folk. It means studying the slaves and the *coloni* attached to the soil along with the ordinary Roman soldiers in the period of the Early Church. We will learn, for instance, that the Roman legions were multi-cultural and multi-colored and some were also Black. It means in the medieval Church studying the serfs bound to the soil, studying the dissidents whom we call heretics, studying that Moorish population in Moslem/Christian Spain, some of whom were brown, some of whom were Black, many of whom were Christian.[4] It means understanding how a Black saint, Benedict the Black (or the Moor) (1526-1589) could arise in multi-ethnic, multi-racial Sicily as a contemporary of Martin Luther.

History from below means studying the beliefs and the spirituality of ordinary people, ordinary religious, and the ordinary clergy. This is why a Church history curriculum might easily have as a component or an elective a course in the history of popular piety. In my opinion, we too easily allow seminarians to dismiss popular piety. In doing so, we too easily separate people from their roots. Our Lady of Guadalupe is a brown-skinned Indian maiden who appeared to a brown-skinned American Indian, Juan Diego, in sixteenth-century

Mexico. She came as one of the poor and the exploited to a people who were poor and exploited. Why was it that it was Black slaves who began to honor Mary as the Virgin of the Apparitions or the *Aparecida* in Brazil and Our Lady of Charity, that is of *El Cobre*, in Cuba? Why is it that the cult of the saints figures so prominently in Santeria ·and in Vodoo? Can anyone honestly study the history of liturgy ignoring the history of popular piety? Our first great liturgical commentator is that marvelously courageous, peripatetic Spanish nun, Egeria, who shows us popular piety evolving into high church liturgy in the streets of Jerusalem at the end of the 4th century. A Jerusalem, by the way, that already showed the racial and cultural diversity of the Church within and without the Roman Empire as all began to converge upon Christianity's favorite pilgrimage center. All of which reminds us, of course, that the Mediterranean Sea was a crossroad for a Roman world of varied colors, cultures, and cross-fertilization, thereby creating a Roman Church that was so rich and variegated in cross-cultural phenomena, that it was known by the second century as catholic.

Today seminary professors are encouraged to stress the pastoral aspect of their courses. We might call this the pastoral perspective. The history of pastoral ministry and the history of evangelization, whether as components of a core course or as electives, bring to the seminarian the reality of history from below. For a long time the history of American pastoral practice has centered along certain well defined themes. All we need do is look at Dolan's study.[5] Here in this two-volume study one will find, I submit, a less than thorough treatment of pastoral activity among Black Catholics on the parish level. Before the Civil War in the South, Black Catholics, slave or free, were to be found in all parishes from New Orleans to Baltimore, St. Augustine to St. Louis. What kind of view of the American Church do we give our students if they do not know that in St. Martinsville, Louisiana, it was taken for granted that a slave had to have his owner's permission to receive communion?[6] What kind of American sacramental theology did we have in this country when it was the regular practice in much of the southern United States for white Catholics to receive communion first and Blacks to receive last? How many who teach pastoral theology know that this venerable custom was maintained until a very recent past? Historically, we like to speak of the American perspective on Church and freedom with John Courtney

Murray and his contribution to political theology. Practically, we should examine that perspective from the viewpoint of parishes in Chicago which were in transition from white to Black, with bitterness and even violence in some neighborhoods. In our history of the American Church, what is the real ecclesiology in a history from below? In fact, in discussing such things as the Immigrant Church and national parishes, whose steeples crowd the skyline of our northern cities, can we ignore, as most surveys often do, the question of all Black parishes in the post-Civil War American Church? If we avail ourselves of oral history—and oral history is a favorite method of practitioners of history from below[7] —we will find out about pastors standing on the church steps, barring entrance to baptized Blacks. This was also a vision of Catholic America that belongs to the very recent past and that affects us still.

Rethinking the Context

I am personally convinced that Church history should be a separate discipline from the history of religious thought or the history of theological thought. I fear that too often we fail to contextualize the religious thought or the theological movement. To put it bluntly, those whose field is abstract thought and speculative reasoning unconsciously seek to drain history of its humanity, its texture, its taste and odors, and its colors.

1993 marked the hundredth anniversary of the Chicago Columbian Exposition. For us who are Catholics, it marks the hundredth anniversary of the Columbian Catholic Congress, the second and last lay Catholic Congress in this country.[8] At the same time, Black Catholics held the Fourth Black Catholic Congress. In a stirring and sometimes eloquent statement, they addressed their fellow Catholics:

> As children of the true Church, we are anxious to witness the extension of our beloved religion among those of our brethren who as yet are not blessed with the true Faith, and therefore we consider it a duty not only to ourselves but to the Church and to God, that we draw the attention of every member of the learned Roman hierarchy to such violation [of racial justice] from Catholic law and Catholic practice....We know that the Roman Church, as she is One and Apostolic, is also Catholic and Holy. With thorough confidence in the rectitude of our course in the enduring love of Mother Church, and the consciousness of our priesthood, we show our devotion to the Church, our jealousy

of her glory and our love for her history in that we respectfully call the attention of the Catholic World, and in particular of the clergy, to those wrong practices which mark the conduct of those of the clergy who have yielded to the popular prejudice.[9]

This statement by Black Catholics at the end of the last century is an expression, I would submit, of "grass-roots" ecclesiology. It is a theology that begins with the premise that the Church's mission is to teach social justice. It is the Church's mission to transform society. It is a Catholic's duty to correct a wrong opinion regarding human rights. These "grass-root" theologians love the Church, admire its history, and are conscious of the priesthood of the laity. They speak about their connection to the Early Church and to the African saints: "…did not the Holy Church canonize Augustine and Monica, Benedict the Moor, Cyprian, and Cyril, Perpetua and Felicity…?" It is a question of African Americans reclaiming for themselves a Catholic identity rooted in the Early Church or in 16th-century Sicily among its African slaves. They did what all Catholic immigrants did…they forged a Catholic identity from the old country, except it was far older than the Middle Ages. What they were in the process of doing, had the process continued, was create a Black Theology. And the pity is, I believe, that for so long American Catholics ignored this aspect of our history…as a Church and as a Catholic people in this section of the world.

Reworking the Goals

One day in the fall of 1853, a woman named Harriet Thompson in New York City sat down at a table and wrote a letter to Pius IX. She was Black, and she was not well educated. No one knows how she got the idea that she could write the pope. No one knows what gave her the idea that the pope would be interested in what she had to say. And perhaps she did not know that her letter would end up in the archives of the Congregation for the Evangelization of Peoples (once called The Propaganda). And she certainly did not know that she would figure in a history book. The letter begins:

Most Holy Father Visible Head of the Church of Jesus Christ, I humbly write these lines to beseech your Holiness in the name of the same Saviour if you will provide for the salvation of the black race in the

United States who is going astray from neglect on the part of those who have the care of souls....[10]

Harriet Thompson proceeds to set forth in a very graphic way the situation of Black Catholics in antebellum New York. She told of an archbishop who, if not hostile, was at least indifferent to the affairs of Blacks. She told of a public school system that openly ridiculed Catholic practices and beliefs.

As soon as the teachers find any children in these schools to be Catholics they teach them directly to protest against the church of God. They tell them that the Blessed Eucharist is nothing but a wafer, that the priest drinks the wine himself and gives the bread to us and that the divine institution of confession is only to make money, and that the Roman pontiff is Anti-Christ.[11]

She speaks about the efforts that Black parents made to enroll their children in the Catholic schools. How they were rebuffed, being told that white children did not wish to go to school with Black children. Some twenty or more signatures of Black men and women are appended to the letter.

I include this incident because this document says something to me about the goals of teaching history in a theological faculty. The first goal is that it be an interesting and moving story. Harriet Thompson could read and write—not too well, with many misspellings and bad punctuation. But in an age of slavery, her literacy was an exception. She was intelligent. The letter is very moving. It's an example of what it means to have the theological virtues of faith and hope. For the letter concludes with the words: "I hope, if it is the will of God for the Black Race to be saved, something will soon take place for the better." She has a keen sense of the rights that Black people had in the Church and how the local bishop ignored those rights. She knew what it meant to have recourse to the Roman See. In this letter we have another perspective on the American Church and on the Holy See, a perspective too easily ignored.

Being a compelling story is important. I believe that in the classroom history should always be first and foremost a compelling account. History is always stranger than fiction. This is part of the reason why, in recent years, historians are saying once again that narrative history has its particular importance.[12] The story helps us remember that history is about people in the midst of events. Harriet Thompson tells us something about the Church as a people...particularly the people others forget. But this story fulfills a second goal for the seminary history professor, which is the need to confront the student with the documents. And in this instance to remind us that the sources of Black Catholic history are still virtually untouched.

That brings me to the third goal of Church history: understanding. The past enables one to understand the present. It helps one to distinguish the strands of the present. The bitterness that existed between certain ethnic groups, who were traditionally Catholic, and American Blacks, are vividly set forth by Harriet Thompson in her letter to the pope. That alignment of ethnic tension still exists in cities like Chicago today.

The fourth goal is breadth. History provides parallels and analogies; it relativizes and it sensitizes. A study of Church history provides a much broader spectrum of cultures and ideas than does a narrowly based national or cultural history. When we curtail the study of history, we curtail our comprehension of the Church as mystery and sacrament.

The fifth goal is to provide a framework for evangelization. The theological notion of inculturation is based upon historical analysis. How do cultures develop, how do they meld with others, how do they survive, how do they die?

Perhaps the final goal should be to provide a background for a theology of Church and for a vision of Church as mystery. One can look at the Church as a social club—a sort of sophisticated chamber of commerce—as a militia, as a family business venture made up of those who are just like us; or as a prophetic sign, an incarnational bridge, a symbol of reconciliation, a sacramental union that makes us pilgrims, climbing through time and space.

Truth and Consequences

All of this sounds well and good. The moment of truth, however, is in the classroom, and that raises certain problems. For the professor, the biggest problem is the constraint of time. How can we include information about African Americans' questions in an already crowded syllabus? How do we cover all of the ethnic bases in a class filled with students as varied as the United Nations? How do we cover the basics at the same time? Perhaps part of the solution is to vary the electives.

A course on American Ecumenism from an historical perspective should include Richard Allen and the African Methodist Episcopal Church. A course on American Catholic Thinkers could easily include Black original thinkers like Daniel Rudd and Thomas Wyatt Turner. A course on Catholic women in the nineteenth century should easily include a segment on Elizabeth Lange, Henriette Delille, or Mathilda Beasley.

There is a consequence to all of this, however. There is the question of student interest. Some seminaries have a representative number of minority students in the enrollment. Some places, however, are as monochrome as cream of wheat. I have stood before classes where the temperature dropped suddenly with no one saying a word when the element of race was introduced into the course. Liberal seminary or conservative, all male or mixed, politically correct or fundamentalist, a classroom of white students in this country can rarely treat race and related issues with equanimity or objectivity. History should provide the perfect background for controversial topics, for distance lends enchantment and age adds a patina that softens the harshness and relieves the glare. Still the ratings show that it is possible for the American public to look at three nights of Alex Haley's *Roots* but not support the longer television series with a Black maid as the heroine with "I'll Fly Away." In that sense, American Catholics from all indications will have the same sensibilities regarding race and the racial environment as the American population in general despite all of our Pastoral Letters and Seminars.

Objectively, the popularity of courses should not be overvalued. Courses taken for personal enrichment are not the same as courses taken for professional knowledge. What is less pleasing is often more valuable. Unless we wish upon future priests and lay ministers a frontal lobotomy that will take away anxiety and remove all tensions, we must allow them to face the spectres and the shades of the past. We can exorcise the demons only when we call their names.

Conclusion

Henri de Lubac once wrote a wonderful book entitled *Catholicism*. I would like to quote one of my favorite passages.

She is the Catholic Church: neither Latin nor Greek, but universal.
Heir to the Catholic goodness of God himself she ever proclaims, as in
St Augustine's time:

"I am in all languages. Greek is mine, Syrian is mine, Hebrew is
mine, [the languages] of all people are mine, for I am the unity of all
peoples. [St Augustine, *Commentary on the Psalms*, PL 37:1929] Nothing authentically human, whatever its origin, can be alien to her. "The
heritage of all peoples is her inalienable dowry." In her, man's desires
and God's have their meeting place....To see in Catholicism one religion among others, one system among others, even if it be added that
it is the only true religion, the only system that works, is to mistake its
very nature, or at least to stop at the threshold. Catholicism is religion
itself. It is the form that humanity must put on in order finally to be
itself. It is the only reality which involves by its existence no opposi-
tion. It is therefore the very opposite of a "closed society."...The Church
is at home everywhere, and everyone should be able to feel himself at
home in the Church. Thus the risen Christ, when he shows himself to
his friends, takes on the countenance of all races and each hears him in
his own tongue.[13]

I like to picture the Church as a very large family living in an ancient, rambling old house with solid foundations, enormous apart-
ments, and a jumble of architectural styles that somehow never clash.
Enormous cellars, musty libraries, huge fireplaces, grand staircases
turning into narrow twisting ladders and sometimes disappearing all
together, bricked-up windows and doorways barely masking the sound
of unseen voices on the other side, meandering corridors, lofty ceil-
ings, narrow cubicles, secret passageways, gorgeous chandeliers, and
marvelous frescoes partly discolored, all of this together found in this
old house. Somehow we all live here, some are here whom we do not
see, some we see but we cannot reach, some are lost and we do not
know how to reach them. But the old house stands, for it was built
on rock.

Notes

[1] See *The Coptic Encyclopedia*, s.v. "Lalibala." The name is often spelled
Lalibela. It is located some 200 miles due north of Addis Ababa.

[2] L. Génicot, "Histoire de l'Église, du Catholicisme, du Christianisme ou de
la Vie Religieuse?" *Revue d'Histoire Écclésiastique*,65 (1970): 68-80.

[3] See Peter Burke, "Overture: the New History, Its Past and Its Future," in
New Perspectives on Historical Writing, ed. by Peter Burke. (University
Park, PA: Pennsylvania State University Press, 1991).

[4]See Verlinden, Charles, *L'esclavage dans l'Europe médiévale.* vol. 1. *Péninsule ibérique, France.* (Brugge: De Tempel, 1955).

[5]Jay Dolan,ed., *The American Catholic Parish. A History from 1850 to the Present.* 2 vols. (New York: Paulist Press, 1987).

[6]See a newspaper clipping in the folder marked "A. Dumartrait to Bishop Blanc, July 10, 1843, St. Martinsville, La., Records of Archdiocese of New Orleans, V-4-0, University of Notre Dame Archives.

[7]See Gwyn Prins, "Oral History," *New Perspectives on Historical Writing.* 114-39.

[8]See *Progress of the Catholic Church in America and the World's Columbian Catholic Congresses,* 2 vols in one. (Chicago: J.S.Hyland, 1897).

[9]Cyprian Davis, O.S.B., "Two Sides of a Coin: The Black Presence in the History of the Catholic Church in America," *Many Rains Ago. A Historical and Theological Reflection on the Role of the Episcopate in the Evangelization of African American Catholics.* (Washington, D.C.: Secretariat for Black Catholics, National Conference of Catholic Bishops. U.S.C.C., 1990.) 49-62. For text, see 57-58.

[10]Harriet Thompson to Pope Pius IX, October 29, 1853, New York. Congregation of the Propaganda Archives. microfilm. *Scritture Riferite nei Congressi: America Centrale,* vol. 16, fols. 770rv, 770rv, 775r, 771rv, 773r, 774r. University of Notre Dame Archives.

[11]Ibid. Spelling corrected in citation.

[12]Peter Burke, "History of Events and the Revival of Narrative," *New Perspectives.* 233-48.

[13]Henri de Lubac, *Catholicism. Christ and the Common Destiny of Man.* (San Francisco:Ignatius Press, 1988. orig. English trans. Turnbridge Wells: Burns and Oates, Ltd., 1950).

Response to Cyprian Davis

Martin Zielinski, Ph.D.
University of St. Mary of the Lake, Mundelein Illinois

Introduction

A number of years ago the Jesuit historian, James Hennessey, was asked to reflect on the role of the church historian in the overall theological enterprise. His initial response was a two word answer: comic relief. Now I don't know what conversations or encounters he may have had which brought forth that comment. His subsequent comments were in a more serious tone than the attention-grabbing two-word answer. In this morning's talk, Cyprian identified a number of key components for teaching church history. In my response, I will begin with two general observations about teaching church history, and then comment on two points from Cyprian's address.

The Cry of the Poor

For the last couple of weeks, while thinking about today's symposium, I found the biblical phrase, "the Lord hears the cry of the poor," running through my mind. Cyprian's emphasis on the history from below and on the importance of narrative history reinforces the power of that biblical phrase for the teaching of church history. When no one else in the world hears the voice of the poor, the Lord listens. My definition of the poor is not restricted to the socio-economic categories. Instead, my understanding of the poor includes those who have a story to tell, but to whom no one listens. The lack of opportunity to tell one's story deprives persons of their dignity. In effect, those denied the opportunity are being told that what they have to say has no value. The role of history and, for our purposes today, church history, is to help the poor tell their story of faith.

One possible implication of this for teaching church history is to expose students to the variety of available resources where the voice of the poor has been recorded. In some cases, the wealth of available resources may be thin but it still exists. Many students believe that nothing is available about this group of people or on this topic. Helping students to "play the detective" can lead them to resources they never imagined existed.

A second implication for helping the poor to tell their story with the assistance of church history relates to the development of pastoral ministry. Students' formal study of church history in the seminary or theological school classroom should develop a sense of historical appreciation in relation to their pastoral ministry. Students should ask: where have they come from, these people I serve in the community? What changes have taken place in the parish to which I am assigned? Who are the oldest members of the parish? What can they tell me about the development of this community of faith?

The pastoral minister must promote the story of faith in the particular community they serve. Time does not permit me to discuss the important area of records management and their preservation for archives, essential resources to help develop the story from below. However, an historical appreciation in pastoral ministry develops out of a willingness to listen to the voices of the present time and past times.

Stories of Faith-Filled Witnesses

My second observation about the teaching of Church history relates directly to the African American Catholic community. My experiences at two parishes on the South side of Chicago and my research on the Catholic Interracial Council of New York provided a deeper appreciation of the faith-filled witnesses of the African American Catholic community. The stories of personal and collective struggles by African American Catholics with the institutional church in the United States offer a powerful witness of fidelity. While not ignoring the fact that racism and discrimination hurt and alienated many African American Catholics, the history of the African American Catholic community provides a lesson for the larger American Catholic Church

When what the Church proclaims to be is at odds with how the Church acts, how does a person of faith respond? The contemporary American Church struggles with this question on many levels. The history of African American Catholics gives poignant examples of fidelity to the universal vision of the Church. In the teaching of

Church history, the stories of these faith-filled witnesses must be told in order for students to understand the struggles of faith and membership. To understand that the theological vision of the Church is more than the particular experience of an individual's relationship to a specific parish, and to be able to arrive at this understanding despite numerous obstacles, proclaims volumes about a depth of faith and personal sanctity. The historical examples of the faith-filled witnesses in the African American Catholic community are rich resources for contemporary theological reflection.

Suggested Addition to the Goals

I found the six goals proposed by Cyprian to be very helpful. As one who often feels frustrated by the time constraints of a quarter system, I must confess that making history a "good story" sometimes seems like the impossible dream. The tension between determining what events students should know as part of the Catholic tradition and what stories to tell about the people is not always kept in balance. Yet each of the goals provides clarity for helping the teachers of Church history develop their art.

One goal comes to mind as a suggested addition to the list. This would be the art of interpretation through the study of Church history. Any number of historical schools provide teachers and students with ways to interpret history. In the specific area of Church history, the art of interpretation should be directed to helping people "read the signs of the times."

The use of Church history as an interpretive tool for reading the signs of the times is not meant to reduce the rigorous demands of scholarship or to reduce the academic integrity of this field. Developing the art of interpretation as a goal of Church history is not just a new juggling of the facts and documents. Developing the art of interpretation is not predetermining conclusions and then seeking evidence to support those conclusions. Developing the art of interpretation is not a call for unwarranted revisionism. I firmly believe, and hope that I practice in the way I teach Church history, that the art of interpretation for Church history should serve as a resource for contemporary Christian life and renewal. This builds upon Cyprian's idea that Church history should provide understanding of the present. Reviving the tradition of the events serves as a resource for contemporary Christian life and renewal. The who, what, when, where, and why of those congresses provided inspiration and direction for the agenda of the recent congresses.

Leo XIII and Truth

During my first year of graduate studies at the Catholic University of America, I developed the habit of copying quotations from what I read, words that really made me stop and think. One of the first that I put down on a 3 by 5 index card was from Pope Leo XIII. He used the quotation in a speech at the opening of the Vatican Archives. The pope drew on a figure from the classical past to describe how these archives should be used. Leo XIII quoted Cicero when he said, "Never let the truth be unsaid and never let untruth be said." The story of the Jesuit Albert Foley writing the life of Bishop Healy showed how difficult it can be for the historian to fulfill Cicero's dictum, especially at a time when people are not willing to hear the truth. Cyprian's comment about allowing people to "face the spectres and shades of the past" connects to this whole issue of truth. Facing historical truths can be an experience of deconstruction and reconstruction. Facing historical truths can make people feel uncomfortable.

A comparison can be made between the facing of historical truth and listening to the words of the Gospel. When we hear the Gospel preached to us, we should feel uncomfortable. The message of the Gospel confronts and challenges the way we live. We know from experience that this leads to growth in our faith life. If the message of the Gospel is to be a challenge for our faith life, then should we be disturbed when this same Gospel-based experience moves into the area of Church history? This harsh reality of the uncomfortable truths that Church history uncovers should not put people on the defensive, put them in a reactive mood, or make them run away. The uncomfortable truths of Church history should make us reflect more deeply, make us act with greater courage to correct injustices, and give us a perspective of humility.

Conclusion

When a master teacher speaks, all in attendance become students. Cyprian Davis is a master teacher and his talk this morning gives nuggets of wisdom gleaned from the field of Church history. Feeling

still like a catechumanate in the field of teaching Church history, I
appreciated the opportunity to listen and respond.

Reading Texts Through Worlds, Worlds Through Texts

Vincent L. Wimbush, Ph.D.
Union Theological Seminary: New York, New York

Introduction

I am honored to have been invited to be a part of this conference. Because I am not Roman Catholic, I cannot exhort you from within that circle or frame of reference, certainly not with respect to spiritual formation and theological education. But because I am African American with a set of experiences generally defining and shaping what is meant by reference to African Americans today, I am able to articulate certain other challenges that I think are important to African Americans generally, and certainly to African Americans interested in the religious life and in forms of ministry, irrespective of church affiliation and orientation. Because I am also by training a biblical scholar, I want to focus those challenges upon the Bible—not upon theological or doctrinal issues, not even upon hermeneutical issues narrowly defined—but upon the social-historical, the political, the phenomenological. In short, I should like to challenge you as an African American and as a Biblical Scholar regarding your understandings of, training in, and engagements of, the Bible. I think such challenges will have implications for the larger issues of spiritual formation, intellectual development and political conscientization and orientation. My challenges have to do not with the interpretation of any text, but with the very notion of texts as religious, mythic texts, as Holy Scripture, with what it means for us to explode the very notion of Holy Scripture, to question the notion of some objective text out there to be interpreted according to some scholar's, church's, or bishop's edict. These challenges aim to help us to think of the imperative not so much as an interpretation of a text, but as an interpretation of the "world."

So I should like to offer some reflections upon what an interpretive history of African Americans' culturalist readings of the Bible might portend for our self-definition and response to the world. I might add that these reflections do not represent anything approaching an exhaustive treatment of primary sources or communities within the African American circle of reference. That my background and bias is Protestant will be evident. But I hope my reflections, though limited and as intellectually as honest as possible, will provide a springboard for discussion of the issues which are of most interest to you.

Cultural Impact on Interpretation

Readings of texts, especially mythic, religious texts, are seldom cultivated by the lone individual; they are generally culturally determined and delimited. The cultural worlds of readers not only determine what texts are to be read, viz., what texts are deemed of value or are included within the canon, how canonical texts are read, and what they mean; they also determine the meaning of "text" itself. Cultural readings are, like cultures themselves, rarely static; they are almost always dynamic and complex. They can, for example, represent, at one time, the struggle of a fledgling nation for self-definition and purpose, and, at another, the rhetorical arsenal for the reform and revitalization of a rather old nation. They can represent for oppressed groups the rhetorics and visions of resistance—against the new or the established nation state. Whatever the character of and motive behind particular readings of mythic and religious texts, such readings are defined, and receive their impetus from, socio-political contexts and circumstances, and in turn function as "readings" of those contexts and circumstances.

No more dramatic and poignant example of the nexus between "readings" of religious texts and the "readings" of world can be found in modernity than in the history of engagement of the Bible by African Americans. Their history of engagement of the Bible not only reflects a particular history of consciousness, but also a provocative hermeneutical challenge, especially regarding an understanding of and response to the "worlds" of the Bible, and the notion of "text" itself. I will discuss further below, but it is important to insert a brief summary of African American biblical interpretation at this point.

African American "Readings" of the Bible

A comprehensive interpretive history of African American "readings" of the Bible remains to be written. Such a history cannot be offered here, but a summary treatment that hints of important developments is in order.

African Americans' engagement of the Bible is a fascinating historical drama. It begins with the Africans' involuntary arrival in the New World that came to be known as the United States. That the drama of the engagement of the Bible among African Americans continues in the present time is a sign of the creativity and adaptability of the African worldview, and of the evocative power of the Bible. From the beginning of their captive experience in what became the United States, Africans were forced to respond to the missionizing efforts of whites. They were challenged to convert to the religions of the slavers. These religions or denominations, supported for the most part by the establishment or the landed gentry, did not have much appeal to the slaves. The formality and the literacy presupposed by the religious cultures of the slavers—in catechetical training and Bible study, for example—clearly undermined efforts to convert the Africans in significant numbers. Not only were the Africans, on the whole—given both custom and law—incapable of meeting the presupposed literacy requirements of these religions, they did not generally seem emotionally disposed toward the general sensibilities and orientations of the devotees, toward their piety and spirituality.[1]

To be sure, the Bible did play a role in these initial missionary efforts. But that role was not primary: its impact was indirect. It was often imbedded within catechetical materials or within elaborate doctrinal statements and formal preaching styles.

The Africans' introduction to "the Bible," or "the Scriptures," by whatever agency in the New World, would have been problematic. Cultures steeped in oral traditions at first think that the concept of religions and religious power circumscribed by a book is frightful and absurd; later they consider them to be awesome or fascinating.[2]

It was not until the late eighteenth century, with the growth of non-establishment, evangelical, camp-meeting revivalistic movements in the north and south that African Americans began to encounter the Bible on a large and popular scale. Attracted by the new evangelicals and revivalists who preached in vivid biblical language and with earnest emotion and fervor, the Africans began to respond enthusiastically and in great numbers. They joined white evangelical camps and began throughout the south and north to establish their own churches and denominational groups. What did not go unnoticed among the Africans was the fact that the white world they experienced tended to explain its power and authority by appeal to the Bible. So they embraced the Bible, transforming it from the Book of the religion of the whites—whether aristocratic slavers or lower class exhorters—into a source both of psychic-spiritual power and of inspiration for learning and affirmation. Biblical language grounded the emergence of an African American religious-language world, a world expressive of strong hopes, including veiled and stinging critiques of slave-holding Christian culture. The narratives of the Old Testament, and the stories of and about Jesus, the persecuted but victorious one, in the New Testament, captured the collective African imagination. This was the beginning of the African American historical encounter with the Bible, and it has functioned as the phenomenological, socio-political, and cultural foundation for the different historical "readings" of the Bible that have followed.

From the late eighteenth century through the late twentieth century, African Americans have continued their "readings" of the Bible. These "readings" reflect major changes and nuances in the self-understandings and orientations of a major segment of African Americans. The founding of the independent churches and denominations beginning in the late eighteenth century historically postdates and logically presupposes the cultivation of certain identifiable African diaspora religious worldviews and orientations. The Bible has played a fundamental role in the cultivation and articulation of such worldviews and orientations. It was rediscovered as a language world full of drama and proclamation such that the slave or freed person could be provided with certain rhetorics and visions.

The most popular "reading" of the Bible developed in the nineteenth century and continued into the twentieth century. According to this "reading," the (Protestant, i.e., mainstream or establishment) canon provided the more aggressive and overtly political rhetorics and visions of prophetic critique against slavery, and the blueprints for "racial uplift," social and political peace, equality and integration as ultimate goal in the era of Jim Crowism and beyond. In addition, steps toward personal salvation were a vital part of the "reading." It reflected the dominant socio-political views and orientations among African Americans in this period. This "reading"—of both the Bible and of American culture—expressed considerable ambivalence: it was both critical and accommodationist. On the one hand, its respect for the canon reflected its desire to accommodate and be included within the American socio-economic-political and religious mainstream. On the other hand, its interpretation of the Bible reflected a social and ideological location "from below" as demonstrated in the blistering critique of Bible-believing, slave holding, racist America. Important personalities—from Frederick Douglass to Martin Luther King, Jr., are among the powerful articulators of this "reading." But the popular sources—the songs, conversion narratives, poetry, prayers, diaries, and the like—most of them anonymous, are a truer, more powerful reflection of history.

It is indisputable that this "reading" reflected considerable ambivalence, on the part of a considerable segment of African Americans, over a long period of history, about their being in America. That it reflects class-specific leanings—and to some extent, perhaps, depending upon the historical period, gender-specific leanings—within the African American population, is also indisputable. Those who continued to "read" the Bible and America in this way continued to hope that some accommodation should and could be made. Those most ardent in this hope saw themselves as close enough to the mainstream to make accommodation (integration) always seem reasonable and feasible.

Historical interest in the dramatic narratives of the Old Testament notwithstanding, there was a certain cluster of passages from the New Testament, especially Galatians 3:26-28 and Acts 2; 10:34-36, that provided both the evocative rhetorical, visionary, and prophetic critique and the hermeneutical foundation for this dominant "mainstream" African American "reading" of Bible—and American culture. These passages were important on account of their emphasis upon hope for realization of the universality of salvation. They were often quoted and paraphrased by generations of African Americans—from the famous to the unknown—in efforts to relate them to the racial situation in the U.S. .

The Major Theme of Late Nineteenth and Early Twentieth Century African American Biblical Interpretation: Racial Unity

Attention to the evocation and engagement of the major theme of one or two of these passages in selected literature is in order. Such attention will not only provide greater clarity about the impetus behind one of the most powerful, if not dominant "readings" of the

Bible and of American culture among African Americans, but will also illuminate the relationships among social location, consciousness and orientation, and interpretive presuppositions and strategies. More specifically, it can help illuminate the complex relationship between the reading of texts and the reading of worlds.

David Walker's famous Article III of his 1829 "Appeal in Four Articles...to the Coloured Citizens of the World," deals with the problem of a religion that frustrates rather than cultivates racial unity and harmony. Throughout the essay he makes clear his understanding of Christianity as mandating racial justice and harmony. Such understanding is the presupposition for both biting prophetic critique against contemporary white Christianity and further cultivation of a type of African American spirituality. Right from the start of this essay, biblical motifs are evident in both quotation and allusion:

> Surely the Americans must believe that God is partial; notwithstanding his apostle Peter declared before Cornelius and others that he has no respect to persons, but in every nation he that feareth God and worketh righteousness is accepted with him.— "The word," said he, "which God sent unto the children of Israel, preaching peace, by Jesus Christ (he is the Lord of all)" [Acts 10:36][3] ...
>
> How can the preachers and people of America believe the Bible? Does it teach them any distinction on account of a man's color? Hearken, Americans! to the injunctions of our Lord and master.... Go ye, therefore, and teach all nations, baptizing them in the name of the Father, and of the Holy Ghost.... " [Matt. 28:19]
>
> I declare, that the very face of these injunctions appears to be of God and not of man. They do not show the slightest degree of distinction.... Can the American preachers appeal unto God, the Maker and Searcher of hearts, and tell him, with the Bible in their hands, that they make no distinction on account of men's colour? [4]

Frederick Douglass (1818-1915), abolitionist and writer, was a most articulate critic of the slave-holding Christianity of his day. His critique was based upon his acceptance of Christianity as a moral force that had particular authority in the debate about slavery and in the construction of a society of racial equality. Douglass embraced the "Christianity of Christ," as he called it, as opposed to morally bankrupt slave-holding Christianity. The former was understood to be "good, pure, holy,...peaceable, and impartial."[5] There is little doubt that the reference to Christianity as "impartial" is most significant.

An allusion to the theme that runs through the New Testament passages quoted at the beginning of this paper, this reference reflects Douglass's (and his world's) conceptualization of the key, defining element for "true" Christianity. Without the emphasis upon impartiality—especially as regards the races—Christianity could not be pure. His inclusion of a parody of slave-holding religion written by a Methodist minister makes clear his and many others' sentiments. The last lines of each stanza, in which the sarcastic reference to "union" occurs, was probably the reason for selection of the piece. It makes the point that Christianity is understood above all to represent the unity of the races, and that it fails most miserably when this unity is undermined:

> Come, saints and sinners, hear me tell
> How pious priests whip Jack and Nell,
> And women buy and children sell,
> And preach all sinners down to hell,
> And sing of heavenly union.
>
> They'll bleat and baa, dona like goats,
> Gorge down black sheep, and strain at motes,
> Array their backs in fine black coats,
> Then seize their Negroes by their throats,
> And choke, for heavenly union.
>
> They'll church you if you sip a dram,
> And damn you if you steal a lamb;
> Yet rob old Tony, Doll, and Sam,
> Of Human rights, and bread and ham;
> Kidnapper's heavenly union.
>
> They'll loudly talk of Christ's reward,
> And bind his image with a cord,
> And scold, and swing the lash abhorred,
> And sell their brother in the Lord
> To handcuffed heavenly union.[6]

The Rhetorical and Social-Critical Character of Late Nineteenth and Early Twentieth Century African American Biblical Interpretations

Reverend Ransom's address entitled "The Race Problem in a Christian State, 1906," may be one of the strongest case examples of the African American reading of the Bible and culture under discussion.

The address focuses upon the racial problem in the United States in the early twentieth century. The perspective is that of an Ohio-born, relatively well educated activist African American clergy. His entire professional life was devoted to "racial uplift." This required, according to Ransom's thinking, leveling prophetic critique against the abuses, weaknesses, and perfidy of both white and African American churches (especially including his own, the African Methodist Episcopal Church).

The address, delivered in a Boston church, is fascinating on a number of scores. First, it fits the genre of public address, functioning as a type of social prophetic critique, befitting an activist cleric. Second, as social critique the address employs a wide range of appropriate and rhetorical strategies, including Enlightenment ideas, references to events in world history, theological argumentation, allusions to denominational doctrine, and loose quotations of and allusions to the Bible. Third, as public address it exhorts and critiques the immediate audience and the United States in general as "the Christian State," with all that such an entity implies for the issues raised.

Racism is of course the primary theme of the address. But it should be noted that racism is defined and accounted for with the use of biblical language. In Ransom's opening statements the biblical notion of the kinship of humanity figures as the historical, theological foundation of Christianity, and is the hermeneutical key to the interpretation of all Scripture and of Christianity:

> There should be no race problem in the Christian State. When Christianity received its Pentecostal baptism and seal from heaven it is recorded that, "there were dwelling at Jerusalem Jews, devout men, out of every nation under heaven. Parthians, and Medes, and Elamites, and the dwellers in Mesopotamia, and in Judea, and Cappadocia, in Pontus and Asia, Phrygia, and Pamphylia in Egypt, and in parts of Libya about Cyrene; and strangers of Rome; Jews and Proselytes, Cretes and Arabians." [Acts 2:5-11a]

> St. Paul, standing in the Areopagus, declared to the Athenians that, "God hath made of one blood all nations of men for to dwell on all the face of the earth." [Acts 17:26]

> Jesus Christ founded Christianity in the midst of the most bitter and intense antagonisms of race and class. Yet he ignored them all, dealing alike with Jew, Samaritan, Syro-Phoenician, Greek and Roman...God,

through the Jew, was educating the world, and laying a moral and spiritual foundation. That foundation was the establishment of the one God idea. Upon this foundation Jesus Christ builded the super-structure of "the Fatherhood of God" and its corollary, "the Brother-hood of man."

The crowning object at which Jesus Christ aimed was, "to break down the middle wall of partition" between man and man," and to take away all the Old Testament laws and ordinances that prevented Jew and Gentile from approaching God on an equal plane. And this He did, "that He might reconcile both unto God in one body by the cross, having slain the enmity thereby, so making peace." [Ephesians 2:14-15][7]

All of the arguments above were applied to the racial situation in the Christian State that was the United States in 1906, "…the first nation that was born with the Bible in its hands."[8] According to Ransom, the Christian State that does not seek to address concretely in the spirit of Jesus the challenge inherent in the ideal of the universal kinship of all humanity—an ideal accepted by the integrationist/accommodationist African American culture, including "mainline" African American churches and a challenge that even became the motto of Ransom's African Methodist Episcopachurch—is a state that has failed to live up to its creed and calling. That the United States had failed so was clear to Ransom.

…the history of our past is well known. The Race problem in this country is not only still with us an unsolved problem, but it consti-tutes perhaps the most serious problem in our country today. In Church and State, from the beginning, we have tried to settle it by compro-mise, but all compromises have ended in failure…. American Chris-tianity will un-Christ itself if it refuses to strive on, until this Race Problem is not only settled, but, settled right; and until this is done, however much men may temporize and seek to compromise, and cry "peace! peace!" there will be no peace until this is done.[9]

The final point Ransom makes is that the Christian State has an obligation to translate its theological heritage and foundations into social and political realities. This should require correspondence be-tween God's transcendence above worldly matters and the Christian state's transcendence over human or worldly, especially racial, acci-dents. This is understood to be the special burden and calling of the

United States, which despite its history of slave holding and its insti-
tutionalization of racial inequality, Ransom sees as a special, inspired
experiment with a divine manifest destiny (very much a squaring
with the political and popular notions—among whites and African
Americans—of the day).

> As God is above man, so man is above race. There is nothing to fear by
> forever demolishing every wall, religious, political, industrial, social,
> that separates man from his brotherman. God has given us a splendid
> heritage here upon these shores; he has made us the pioneers of human
> liberty for all mankind. He has placed the Negro and white man here
> for centuries, to grow together side by side...thus will these two peoples
> one at last become the school masters of all the world, teaching by
> example the doctrines of the brotherhood of man. If the new Jerusa-
> lem tarries in its descent to earth, coming down from God out of heaven,
> then we, not like some foolish tower-builders upon the plains of Shinar,
> but taught from heaven in a better way, shall build upon the teachings
> of Jesus, with the doctrine of human brotherhood as taught by Him,
> until fraternity realized, shall raise us to the skies.[10]

Ransom's address is an interpretation of the world that he experienced in the early part of the twentieth century: postslavery, post-
war urban America sometimes, in some places, struggling with the
racial problems, most times, in too many places, ignoring the racial
problems altogether. Ransom himself was a part of the relatively privileged class among African Americans—with access to some educational opportunities, with some independence, on account of location within a relatively less oppressive urban environment, and his
reading of the world was class- and race-specific. The goal of full
integration within American society made sense to those who defined themselves as those in the middle—close, but not close
enough— to the acceptable type of American citizen.

People appealed to the Bible, as one of the most important sources
of authority, in order to persuade different publics of the wisdom of
the course of integration, the acceptance of all human beings as part
of the American experiment. This way of using the Bible was unique
neither in American history nor in Ransom's time, especially in the
context of discussions about racial matters. But clearly Ransom's position reflected a particular type of engagement of the Bible that assumed the key to its mysteries to be the truth of including all human
beings within God's economy.

So as Ransom used the Bible to read his world, to interpret and critique it, he also reflected a particular type of reading of the Bible. It reflected heightened consciousness of social location as determinant of engagement.

Despite arguments to the contrary, the Bible has not only been important among Roman Catholics, but has also functioned among other groups as a rhetorical, political, and ideological playing field. I challenge you to recall from the proceedings of the First Colored Catholic Congress which met in Washington, D.C., January 1-3, 1889, some of the rhetoric on the part of both Africans and whites.

In an opening sermon, Cardinal Gibbons, a leading Irish American Catholic prelate, offered these exhortations:

> Remember the eye of the whole country is upon you....It is not so much social position that makes the man, but the manner in which he exercises his liberty....
>
> Resolve to unite with your pastors in promoting every good cause; you belong to a church which knows no north, no south, no east, no west. no race, no color, one which even the civil war could not divide, a church which knows not Jew, Greek or Barbarian. Our Saviour broke down the wall that divided men and made us one family; we know no race...[Eph.2].[11]

Notice the striking rhetorical use of Gal. 3:26f and Ephesians 2 to promote African allegiance and obedience. But notice also the use of the Bible—in fact, some of the same references—on the part of Daniel Rudd, the lay African American Catholic delegate and publisher, who was voted permanent chair of the Congress in recognition of his initiation and founding of the Congress movement:

> ...the Catholic Church marks at every milestone, the first and only genuine effort to prove the Fatherhood of God, and the brotherhood of man.... [These ideals] are enunciated by the Catholic Church in no doubtful terms. In the Catholic Church mankind [is] reunited and the promise redeemed.[12]

Given the circumstances, the fact that there was then no possibility for a radically separate gathering for African American Catholics, these sentiments—admittedly through the coolest rhetoric, according to my Protestant, left-wing, low church Reformation background and sensibilities—suggest in the thinking the imperative of the Catholic Church realizing within its ranks the ideal of equality. The muted rhetoric may reflect not only the limitations of gaining space for separatist African American thinking and deliberation according to Catholic polity, but also the place of Roman Catholicism within the American religious, social, and cultural life of the times.

For my purposes in arguing, what is most important to note is the difference in the role or function of the Bible within the one church communion that was Catholicism. This role is not doctrinal or theological; it is rhetorical and political.

The Primacy of Social Location in Biblical Interpretation
The Bible may have been a most welcome and powerful ally of Ransom and others during the nineteenth century and into the early part of the twentieth century. But what remains to be explained is how this could have happened, how the likes of Frederick Douglass, David Walker, Reverend Ransom, and many other women and men of color could come to embrace the Bible in the first place. This is not now the question about the mere historical events (Great Awakenings, founding of African American churches and sub-denominational groups) leading up to the works and careers of those discussed. The question is rather about how the phenomenon of African Americans coming to engage the Bible developed at all. How can a people by tradition and sensibility steeped in oral tradition make the step toward psychic acceptance of a Book as source of authority and power and spirituality? How does a people enslaved by a people of a Book come to accept that Book as authoritative and legitimate? How can a people come to interpret their experiences in the world through a Book (with its narratives and codes) that has little to do with their own origins and immediate historical experiences? Again, the question is not about the mere historical events or antecedents; it is about phenomenological and psychic changes.

The most defensible explanation lies in a meeting of "worlds." African Americans found positive and constructive ways of viewing their "self in the world" similar to the views of "self in the world" in the variety of "worlds" found in the Bible. With its arresting and repeated stories of underdogs surviving and conquering, and the ultimate story of a Savior figure who is mistreated but who ultimately triumphs in the New Testament, it is little wonder that African Americans came to embrace the Bible. This was so not simply because of the proselytizing efforts and successes among whites or African Americans, but because African Americans identified with the protagonists of the biblical dramas. Again and again the real situations of the heroes and heroines of the Bible appeared to be similar to those of the historical experiences of most African Americans. The oppressed of the New World heard themselves being described in the stories of the Bible. The Africans in the New World applied to themselves the inclusion of all humanity within the economy of God. Only by assuming some such phenomenological event can we find help explaining how the likes of Douglass and others could engage the Bible. Only by understanding it now not as the road map to nation building but as a manifesto for the oppressed and the marginal could such persons have been taken up the Bible. Only by assuming a hermeneutic of and from the perspective of the racially oppressed can we explain the history of African American engagement of the Bible. Only such a hermeneutic explains the particular version or gloss upon the historical engagements of African Americans made by those figures discussed above. Their positions make sense only to the extent in which they can be placed in the middle—between white (Protestant) mainline culture and sensibilities, and African marginal culture and sensibilities. The African American history of engagement with the Bible suggests the power and challenge of the nexus between social location and biblical interpretation, and of a consistent hermeneutic "from below." African Americans, by virtue of their dramatic history, challenge every reading of the Bible to be more honestly and explicitly (and provocatively) a reading of a world.

Even as African American religious history establishes the strength of the connection between social location and interpretation, it also makes clear that the very notion of "text" undergoes a change: if the core or foundational hermeneutic among African Americans is, as I have suggested, primarily defined by commitment to defining the African presence in the New World—with *radical inclusiveness*, from below or from without, emerging *as the dominant principle* argued and advocated by the majority of the African American religious— then there really is no separate "text" "out there" with assumed universal authority; there is primarily a language and image world, a world of stories that dramatize this dominant principle (and explanatory words) necessarily accepted on account of life situation, a dominant principle personified by characters within that language world, a dominant principle by which the Christian God, the Christian Savior figure, and Christian traditions generally are judged. Only on the basis of commitment to these principles can the African Americans' "conversion" to Christianity be understood. and their engagement of that part of the tradition that is Holy Book be understood. The latter was fundamentally changed from "text"—understood as static source of eternal truth that required a certain authority (intellectual or ecclesiastical or doctrinal) to be engaged—to a language world that could easily, freely, with much creative play, be engaged "from below," or from the margins. Taking the Holy Book off its repository-of-truth pedestal was a radical phenomenological event and challenge, given the status of African Americans and the respect accorded to reading in the American culture.[13] To view the Holy Book as full of stories illustrating the truth about the radical inclusiveness of God's economy of salvation was to explode the notion of canon as it was understood. Not meanings of texts, but interpretations of world, of socio-political and cultural events, became primary; texts functioned to supply rhetorics and images, helping African Americans—in the way of a prism—to see themselves and the world in different colors. The Bible became important because it was received as "world" that could interpret "world." The contribution of African American religious traditions to hermeneutical theory is its modeling of a radical and consistent adherence to the primacy of interpretation (determination) of everything through "world."

Conclusion

I can conclude by arguing that, because of the politics involved, we ought no longer think of interpretation of the Bible as the objective or true meaning that can be accessed either through historical-critical scholarship or through ecclesiastical pronouncements. We must think of it in terms of "worlds" interpreting "worlds," and "texts" interpreting "texts." Only then can we begin to think seriously about ideological freedom.

Notes

[1] Janet D.Cornelius, "When I Can Read My Title Clear." In *Literacy, Slavery, and Religion in the Antebellum South* (Columbia: University of South Carolina Press,1991): Chapter 4.

[2] Sam D. Gill, "Nonliterate Traditions and Holy Books: Toward a New Model." In *Holy Books in Comparative Perspective*, eds. Rodney Taylor and W. Denny. (Columbia: University of South Carolina Press, 1985): 226f.

[3] Milton C. Sernett, ed. *Afro-American Religious History: A Documentary Witness* (Durham: Duke University Press,1985): 191-92.

[4] Sernett, 194.

[5] Sernett, 104.

[6] Sernett, 107.

[7] Sernett, 296-97.

[8] Sernett, 297.

[9] Sernett, 298.

[10] Sernett, 304.

[11] Daniel Rudd, *Three Catholic Afro-American Congresses*. Repr. (New York: Arno Press, Inc., 1978): 10.

[12] Rudd, 25.

[13] Rhys Isaac, "Books and Social Authority of Learning: The Case of Mid-Eighteenth Virginia." *Printing and Society in America*. Ed. William L. Joyce, David D. Hall, and Richard D. Brown, et al. (Worcester MA: American Antiquarian Society,1983): 230f. Gill, 224-28.

Response to Vincent L. Wimbush

Diane Bergant, C.S.A., Ph.D.

Catholic Theological Union: Chicago, Illinois

Introduction

First let me thank Professor Wimbush for an informative and challenging paper. My remarks are not intended to be merely responses to his paper, but to point to some of the issues, content, and method contained therein that might be integrated as constitutive, not peripheral, components of my own biblical method and pedagogy.

Biblical studies has witnessed a growing interest in the use of the human sciences for the investigation of Scripture. This is not surprising, since theology develops out of socio-cultural reality. One such approach employs sociological categories and/or models in an attempt to elicit meaning from the socio-cultural reality of the original community. Examples of this approach include Norman Gottwald's *The Tribes of Yahweh* (Maryknoll: Orbis Books, 1979) and *The Hebrew Bible: A Socio-Literary Introduction* (Philadelphia: Fortress Press, 1985), Bruce Malina's *The New Testament World: Insights from Cultural Anthropology* (Atlanta: John Knox Press, 1981), and *Christian Origins and Cultural: Practical Models for Biblical Interpretation* (Atlanta: John Knox, Press, 1986). Recognizing the interpretive influence of unexamined preunderstanding, another approach is more concerned with identifying the social location of the reader. Examples of this approach include *Stony the Road We Trod: African American Biblical Interpretation,* edited by Cain Hope Felder (Philadelphia: Fortress Press, 1991) and *The Bible and the Politics of Exegesis,* edited by David Jobling, Peggy L. Day, and Gerald T. Sheppard (Cleveland: Pilgrim Press, 1991). Professor Wimbush's paper is an example of this second approach.

I have organized my comments under three categories: issues, content, method. I will first mention what Professor Wimbush says relative to each point and then discuss the role that his insights might play in my own work.

Issue: The Influence of One's Social Location and
Worldview in Biblical Interpretation

The over-arching issue of the paper is the critical role that social location plays in biblical interpretation. While the focus here is on African American concerns, if we do not admit that every interpreter speaks from a particular worldview, we might be led to think that Professor Wimbush's emphasis is interesting but atypical. The question of social location raises a twofold pedagogical challenge. Students should realize that, contrary to a view held by some, there is no purely objective way of looking at things. No one is free of the heritage (religious, national, racial, ethnic, political, etc.) that has shaped her or his worldview. This heritage has predisposed judgments, called forth values, and actually shaped the way reality is perceived. The several cultures that each of us claims have played a significant role in fashioning our worldview. We possess many of the features of these cultures and we carry the effects of their histories. The pedagogical challenge then is: 1) to help students to read biblical interpretation with an appreciation for the insights of the interpreter yet realizing that these insights originate from and, most likely, support the worldview of that interpreter. This does not invalidate the interpretation; it merely situates it within its proper yet circumscribed context; 2) to help students to uncover the features of their own social location, thus enabling them to appreciate their particular perspectives as valuable yet limited.

Content: The African American Reading
Underscores the "Universality of Salvation"

The essay itself is essentially a short history of African American encounter with and subsequent interpretation of the Bible, a history that is seldom if ever a part of the history of interpretation found in most text books or biblical dictionaries. Professor Wimbush points to 'the universality of salvation' as the hermeneutical key that has opened the Bible to the African American community. This key, which is biblical in origin, has both reproached the racist Christian state and enlivened the oppressed communities. Pedagogically, it is important for students to realize that the standard histories of interpretation are both limited and biased, and that histories such as that sketched here should be included in their study, not to replace but to modify biased conventional perspectives. While such inclusion of historical information may well instill pride in students of various ethnic or racial backgrounds, the reason for doing this is not some subtle form of condescension but historical accuracy and intellectual integrity.

Method: Hermeneutical Preference—Reading the text "From Below"

What most interests me about this paper is the method described and demonstrated. The title of the paper, "Reading Texts Through the Worlds and Worlds Through Texts," is itself a concise description of that method: texts are read from the perspective of the world of the reader, and the world of the reader is perceived through the lens of the text. While I have adopted such an approach myself, one point stressed by Professor Wimbush threw light on my own unexamined preunderstanding. He insisted that not only should the text and the world of the interpreter be critiqued, but the history of interpretation should be examined as well. With the exception of the area of feminist concerns, I have not always done this. It has become clear that I must exercise the hermeneutic of suspicion more extensively.

The short overview of history in this article shows that the African American community has consistently recontextualized the biblical tradition in order to resignify it. "They embraced the Bible, transforming it from the Book of the religion of the whites—whether aristocratic slavers or lower class exhorters—into a source of psychic-spiritual power, a source of inspiration for learning and affirmation. Biblical language grounded the emergence of an African American religious language world expressive of strong hopes including veiled and stinging critiques of slave-holding Christian culture." This approach 'from below' was historically both critical and accommodationist. Because of the repressive situations to which African Americans sere subjected, the critique was veiled and the interpretation understandably restrained. However, such a cryptic or coded strategy should be unnecessary today. We have entered an era of openness, respect, and cooperation, when the creative techniques and insights of one social group can enhance the techniques and insights of another. Today, the African American critique must be heeded and its interpretation must be candid. Only in such openness can an African American perspective itself be sharpened by critical exchange with other interpretive approaches and, at the same time, make a unique contribution to the entire hermeneutical enterprise. In light of all of this, professors of biblical studies, through their own teaching and through the writings of African American scholars, should both acquaint their students with various methods of cultural hermeneutics and enable students to engage in biblical interpretation consistent with their own social location.

The African American Experience and U.S. Roman Catholic Ethics: "Strangers and Aliens No Longer?"

Bryan Massingale, S.T.D.
St. Francis Seminary: Milwaukee, Wisconsin

Introduction

The philosopher Immanuel Kant declared that the interests of our reason could be summarized in three questions: "What can I know? What ought I to do? What may I hope?"[1] Ethics concerns itself with the second of these questions, attempting through the use of reason, insight, and intuition, through sustained reflection, disciplined argumentation, and passionate discussion, to answer the question, "What ought I to do?" For Christians, this pursuit of the obligatory good is also impacted decisively by the reality of faith, of a life-shaping commitment to the God of Jesus Christ. Thus in the Christian context a two-fold ethical question emerges: "What sort of persons should we become because we believe in Christ?" "What sort of actions should we perform because we believe in Christ?"[2] The moral theologian, then, seeks to explore the implications of Christian belief for human behavior.

Consequently, for Christians the ethical question is a theological concern as well. Here a critical observation must be made concerning the contextual character of theological thought. Theological reflection is a human activity whose questions and modes of analysis are conditioned by the cultural resources and social interests of those who engage in it. Paraphrasing an insight of the African American theologian, James Cone, the social and cultural environment of a people in a large measure determines the kinds of religious questions they ask.[3] Thus it follows that for Christians, the nature of the ethical good—how we speak of it and how we conceive of it—is conditioned and affected by the social, cultural, and historical situation in which we find ourselves.

For African Americans (and white Americans as well, though for different reasons to be explored later) the historical circumstance which most decisively affects the ethical quest is the reality of racism, that is, the existence of an unequal distribution of power, privilege, and prestige based upon race—and the beliefs and strategies used to justify and defend such unbalanced distribution.[4] Racism has constantly and consistently stymied the quest of black Americans for justice, acceptance, and equal access to social, political, and economic opportunity. This assertion that ethical pursuits and reflection are influenced by the reality of racism is not meant to deny either the diversity of the black community or the pluralism present in the black experience. That is, many other factors also influence or condition African American perceptions of the moral enterprise, not the least of these being gender and class. Such factors notwithstanding, the experience common to all visible African Americans is the rejection, humiliation, lack of acceptance, and otherwise pejoratively differential treatment which stems from the dominant culture's insidious, pervasive, albeit largely unarticulated, belief that most blacks are intellectually, culturally, and morally inferior to whites.[5]

Hence, the chief contention of this paper is that our conception, articulation, and realization of the good is affected to no small degree by the color-consciousness of North American (and European) theology and ethics.[6] Indeed, in light of the conclusion reached by the Kerner Commission nearly a quarter of a century ago, namely, that "race prejudice has shaped [American] history decisively,"[7] Americans cannot pursue the ethical quest or address moral issues with integrity and responsibility without being attentive to the reality of racism. Hence, a critical question emerges which is seldom averted to: How can we conceive of and speak about the behavioral implications of the Christian faith in a community of discourse and reflection which is marred by racial prejudice, malice, ignorance, indifference, and deception?

This paper aims to provide some initial insights and perspectives into this question. To this end, this essay will examine the response of U.S. Catholic moral theologians to the reality of racism, the dominant features and characteristics of African American religious ethics, and finally, the convergence which can exist between Catholic moral theology and African American ethical tenets and convictions. My aim is to initiate a dialogue between the African American experience and Catholic ethics. An underlying concern will be the influence of social location upon one's understanding and appreciation of the good.

I. U.S. Catholic Ethics and the African American Experience

I will confine this examination to those reflections developed by Catholic moralists in the United States, for these participate in the community of discourse shaped by the American experience of racial prejudice in a way that magisterial statements originating in Rome do not. Our attention will be directed to two principal sources. The first are the "Notes on Moral Theology" which appear annually (up to 1970, on a semi-annual basis) in *Theological Studies* (1940-present). This journal is widely recognized as the premier publication of the American theological community, and its yearly comprehensive surveys of the moral literature are without parallel in the English-speaking world. The second source are the published Proceedings of the annual meetings of the Catholic Theological Society of America (1946-present). As this association is the principal professional organization of American Catholic moralists, its reports give us a fair measure of the scholarly interests of this group. These two sources taken together provide a representative sampling of the dominant concerns of American Catholic moralists. We should keep in mind that our interest is not in the activity of the broad field of theology; rather it is specifically focused on the attention given by U. S. Catholic ethicists to the African American experience and matters of racial justice.

A. "Notes on Moral Theology," Theological Studies (1940-present)

The principal conclusion to be drawn from a survey of the "Notes" can be expressed in the words of one of their authors, Robert H. Springer, who in 1970 wrote:

> In combing through the journals for material for these Notes with an eye open for theology and race, it came as a disappointment to discover how little there is to report. One's first reaction is to drop the topic from the survey. On second thought it seems better to report the meager findings and call this to the attention of the moral fraternity....[8]

Unfortunately, I must report that Springer's summons to the moral "fraternity" has gone unheeded. A review of the "Notes" from 1970 to the present reveals virtually no mention of—and certainly no sustained attention to—the reality of racism or race relations.[9] One searches the "Notes" in vain for in-depth reflection on events such as the Black Power Movement, the open housing marches, the debates over affirmative action, or the racial conflagrations of 1965, 1967, and 1968. Thus the Civil Rights Movement, the catalyst for some of the most epochal social changes in U.S. history, passed unnoticed by American Catholic moralists who were consumed by other matters—specifically, the controversies surrounding the morality of artificial contraception.

What treatment one does find of race relations in these "Notes" is limited to the period of the late 1940s and 1950s. The first mention is found in 1948. Here, Gerald Kelly summarizes an article which brands racial discrimination as "unjust, impious, and scandalous." Kelly then goes on to treat the question of whether the Sunday Mass obligation ceases for the Negro who is excluded from the local "white" church. While he acknowledges that such ecclesial discrimination is unjust and "harmful to the Negro's spirit" and Catholicity, Kelly nonetheless concludes that "it does not of itself excuse him from hearing Mass. That question must be solved on the basis of the difficulty of getting to another church." Finally, Kelly considers the moral obligation of whites to render to blacks what the moralists term *communia signa dilectionis*, that is, common signs of love and respect. Here Kelly concludes that white people are morally obliged to render such ordinary civil courtesies and respect to black people, noting that refusal to do so "is a sin against charity."[10]

I cite this article at some length because it illustrates well the standard treatment which racism receives when it is mentioned in the "Notes."[11] There is a general recognition of the moral evil of compulsory racial segregation,[12] but no call to attack or dismantle this unjust social system. Rather, the moralists typically appeal to the charity—not the sense of justice[13]—of whites, calling upon individuals to manifest courtesy and respect in their personal dealings with African Americans. After the issuance of the Supreme Court's desegregation decision of 1954, there is a treatment of the duty of Catholics to respect the law, but no recognition that believers are called to be proactive agents in the achievement of racial justice.[14]

Before we take leave of the "Notes," one should appreciate that although the moral examination of racism during this early period now may appear quaint and inadequate, at least the moralists of the late forties and fifties in some way averted to this topic. After 1963, with the exception of Springer's appeal in 1970 that Catholic ethicists pay more attention to this subject, the theme of racial justice all but disappears from this moral survey.

B. The Proceedings of the
Catholic Theological Society of America (1946-present)

The records of the yearly convocations of U.S. Catholic theologians reveal a similar pattern of omission and neglect with regard to racial concerns. A survey of the *Proceedings* from 1946 to 1972 yields only two extensive examinations of the American race question.[15] The first of these, written in 1958 on the morality of segregated education (note *four* years after the historic decision of Brown vs. Board of Education)[16] is particularly interesting for illustrating the manner in which theologians approached the ethical issues involved. The author, Francis Gilligan, begins with the common teaching of the moralists that the state could for reasons of public peace and safety restrict the civil liberties not only of individuals but even of groups of persons. He then observes that the "fundamental reason" for the existence of segregated schools "is the discomfort and unhappiness the white person experiences when he is forced to attend the same schools with Negroes." He then notes that since human beings are entitled to "a reasonable amount of happiness," some theologians teach that if one experiences "a grave inconvenience or unpleasantness" in fulfilling an affirmative precept, one may be excused from complying with it.[17] Thus is the case of those who resist the mandates for school desegregation. Gilligan concludes, however, that the practice of racial segregation in education was "immoral" for three reasons: 1) the feelings of Negroes must also be considered, feelings of resentment, humiliation, dishonor, and inferiority; 2) the inevitability of eventual integration since, as a practical matter, "the Negroes cannot be kept in a permanent quarantine;" and 3) the international situation, i.e., the need to keep the non-Caucasian peoples of India, Africa, and the Orient from moving into the sphere of Communism.[18]

In the discussion which followed this presentation, the eminent moralist, John Ford, made a very interesting intervention. He agreed that segregation is unjust and "a violation of commutative justice,"

that is, a failure to give people the necessary honor to which all people
are by right entitled. However, he observed:

> the doctrine of Christ inculcates more insistently the notion that we
> should give rights in commutative justice; nowhere does Christ en-
> courage us to fight for what is our due. It would be better for theolo-
> gians and priests generally to preach to whites that they should give
> rights due to the Negroes, rather than to urge the Negroes to press for
> the rights that are their due. Otherwise we might be encouraging fights
> and violence.[19]

What is especially noteworthy is the suggestion that despite the
judgment that racial segregation (at least in the sphere of education)
was unjust, the solution lies in encouraging whites to yield or con-
cede rights to blacks, rather than in encouraging blacks to press for
what is their due (as in the Civil Rights Movement). As an African
American, I cannot help but notice that in Catholic moral discourse,
blacks are treated as the *objects* of white study, analysis, and charity—
and rarely seen as *subjects* capable of independent action or creative
initiative which can shape white response. To put it another way,
there is no acknowledgment of black *agency*, black people are usually
acted upon, seldom the actors, in Catholic moral discourse. Such a
view cannot but render Catholic ethical reflection in matters of race
inadequate and impoverished, if not absolutely erroneous.

This view of blacks as the objects of white study and analysis is also
present in the 1963 contribution of Joseph Leonard. What makes
this article noteworthy is his forthright acknowledgment that the
silence of the Church on matters of racial justice is itself "the most
theologically involved problem." Indeed Leonard declares:

> Historically it is impossible to deny that from the end of the Civil War
> until modern times, an almost universal silence regarding the moral
> issues involved in segregation blanketed the ecclesiastical scene. The
> American hierarchy and theologians remained mute, and this at a time
> when...enforced segregation was growing and extending more and more
> into all areas of life.[20]

The author continues by stating that this silence, inattention, and
neglect stemmed from not only a disinterest in the state of the Negroes and a timidity in the face of entrenched social mores, but also
from a widespread acceptance of the technical distinction between

"discrimination" (which was judged immoral) and "segregation" (which was immoral provided that equal facilities were not available). Thus Leonard asserts: "What was lacking was the knowledge and the realization that all enforced and compulsory racial segregation was discrimination...[T]he distinction—no matter how valid speculatively—was not valid in practice."[21] One can only wonder if greater awareness of and openness to the black experience of reality—in short, an appreciation of black subjectivity and agency—would have hastened this realization.

It was not until 1974 that an African American Catholic, Joseph Nearon, addressed the CTSA.[22] And it comes as no surprise that he concluded:

> The "racism" of American Catholicism is, in my opinion, above all a question of omission.... On the level of theology and theological reflection the black experience has been considered irrelevant—or perhaps, more accurately—until blacks began to press the issue American Catholic theologians never adverted to the fact that the black experience might offer a datum for theological reflection.... Catholic theology is racist. If this fact can be blamed on the cultural situation, if it is more the result of omission and inattention than to conscious commission it is still a fact. There is an insensitivity here which can only remain blameless until it has been pointed out and I serve notice to you, my colleagues, that I am now pointing it out. I hasten to add that I do this not to condemn, but to awaken.[23]

Sadly however, I must report that Fr. Nearon's "wake-up call" has gone unheeded by American Catholic moralists. While the CTSA *as a whole has* made conspicuous efforts in recent years to be attentive to the African American experience, such as sponsoring a continuing seminar devoted to African American Catholic theology, this same responsiveness is not evidenced in the field of moral theology. In 1982, at the organizational gathering of the first on-going continuing seminar in moral theology, those in attendance identified "the most important areas" within the discipline "in need of exploration and research" by American Catholic moralists. Issues of bioethics, war and peace, the influence of feminism, sexual ethics, the relationship between personal and social justice, and the role of authority were offered. Noteworthy by its absence is any mention of race relations, racism, or racial justice.[24] A survey of the topics of the moral seminars since that initial meeting shows a similar omission and inattention. To date, not a single moral seminar has been devoted to racial topics. One can only conclude that issues of race relations and racial justice are not pressing or significant concerns for American Catholic ethicists.

In concluding this survey, it would be an injustice to ignore the exceptions which exist to this pattern of omission, silence, neglect, and indifference to racial concerns in the U.S. Catholic moral academy. One cannot overlook the efforts of John La Farge, Joseph Leonard, and Daniel Maguire.[25] Nor should one fail to mention the 1979 pastoral letter of the U.S. Bishops on racism, *Brothers and Sisters to Us*.[26] Yet, such works are truly the "exceptions which prove the rule." Thus, the conclusion is obvious and inescapable: the moral aspects of race relations have not been, and still are not, a major concern or significant interest of American Catholic ethicists. Documentable history does not support any other judgment. Indeed, to state that racial justice is of peripheral interest to the moral academy may well be an overstatement. Hence, the task or goal of establishing a dialogue between the African American experience and U.S. Catholic moral theology has to surmount a major difficulty: the lack of a dialogue partner…indeed, the absence of any significant evidence of interest on the part of Amerlcan Catholic ethicists in what is arguably the most persistent and insidious human rights issue in America.[27]

II. Characteristics of African American Religious Ethics
We now commence a delineation of the principal ethical convictions and tenets derived from the African American experience as articulated by theologians rooted in that experience.[28] We seek to discover the major themes which permeate African American ethical discourse in order to discover what might emerge as common ground for a conversation with Roman Catholic ethical reflection.

A. The Fundamental Principle: Universal Inclusion
Peter J. Paris, an African American social ethicist, provides a cogent presentation of the fundamental moral principle and conviction which animates and permeates the ethical reflection of black Americans:

> The tradition that has always been normative for the black churches and the black community is not the so-called Western Christian tradi-

tion per se, although this tradition is an important source for blacks. More accurately, the normative tradition is that tradition governed by the principle of nonracism which we call the black Christian tradition. *The fundamental principle of the black Christian tradition is depicted most adequately in the biblical doctrine of the parenthood of God and the kinship of all peoples[.]... The doctrine of human equality under God is...the final authority for all matters pertaining to faith, thought, and practice.*[29]

In other words, the constitutive, essential, and distinctive character-istic of African American religious ethics is an emphatic insistence upon and unreserved commitment to the principle of the freedom and equality of *all* persons under God. It is difficult, nay impossible, to overstate the centrality of this norm in the black religious experi-ence. Paris maintains that this doctrine is "the essence of the black Christian tradition"[30] and thus declares, "In short, its function in the black experience is categorical, that is, it is unconditional, absolute, and universally applicable."[31]

A survey of the works of other leading black religious ethicists also reveals the essential character of this primary commitment to the equal dignity of all human beings under God. It is the signal feature of the ethical thought of black Harvard ethicist Preston Williams. In an authoritative article, Williams writes: "The Afro-American moral perspective makes central the belief in the common origin and hu-manity of individuals and thus their sacredness and equality."[32]

The corpus of Williams's writings demonstrates his commitment to this principle as fundamental to his own perspective. Indeed, it is the central norm for his vision of social life and critique of social policies:

> Black response to enslavement, oppression, disenfranchisement, dis-crimination, and other forms of racist social structure has traditionally been a call toward inclusive and open community structures. In gen-eral Black response to white racism has not involved a *quid pro quo* retaliation toward past and present injustice.... [In the words of Dr. Williams]: "Suffice it to say that most black visions of a racially and socially just community stem from the desire on the part of blacks to be counted as equal, fully person, and citizen, in the human family *and to have all others similarly counted.*[33]

Finally, the noted black intellectual, Harvard professor Cornel West, demonstrates how this principle is so absolute and fundamental that it functions as a prophetic critique of the African American community's own internal affairs. It is the basis for West's unsparing critique of the existence of sexism and homophobia in the black community. Repeatedly, West insists that the process of social change in the black community must have a moral foundation rooted in a pervasive commitment to the dignity of all peoples, a commitment to name the truth and to do the truth, sparing no one, not even black folk or kin.[34] In other words, what is expressed time and again in the black ethical perspective is an insight so well-articulated by Martin Luther King, Jr., "Injustice anywhere is a threat to justice everywhere."[35]

In sum, the foremost, bedrock principle of African American ethical reflection and sensibility is an existential and core commitment to a conviction which other Christian bodies may espouse in a merely rhetorical manner: the equal dignity of all peoples in the sight of God. For black Christians, this is not an abstract idea but a "normative condition" and "the most fundamental requirement" of faith commitment.[36] In the words of the African Methodist bishop C. M. Tanner, written at the turn of the century:

> We preach, stand for and practice the truth that all men the white, the red, the yellow, the brown, the black, are all and are to the same extent, our brothers. We claim that there is but one race in the sight of God, the human race, and the blackest and the whitest are brothers. This we strive to hold, not as a mere high sounding, general statement, but as a great truth of which we seek to make practical application at every opportunity that presents itself.[37]

B. A Passionate Concern for Justice

Flowing from this emphatic insistence upon the equality of dignity present in the human family, African American religious ethics is impassioned about the pursuit of justice, especially for those who are excluded from practical membership in the human community: the weak, the helpless, the downtrodden, the despised. Black ethicists evidence an acute attention to the cries of those who are silenced and rendered invisible by social forces—in particular that of racism. The African American ethic is tireless and vehement in making manifest the systemic flaw of American society: justice is not granted to all—indeed, America has failed to honor its promise to grant "life, liberty, and the pursuit of happiness" to all of its citizens.

The words of Martin Luther King, Jr., provide eloquent witness of this feature of the black ethic:

> In a sense we've come to our nation's capital to cash a check. When the architects of our republic wrote the magnificent words of the Constitution and the Declaration of Independence, they were signing a Promissory note to which every American was to fall heir....
>
> It is obvious today that America has defaulted on this promissory note in so far as her citizens of color are concerned. Instead of honoring this sacred obligation, America has given the Negro people a bad check; a check which has come back marked "insufficient funds." We refuse to believe that there are insufficient funds in the great vaults of opportunity of this nation. And so we've come to cash this check, a check that will give us upon demand the riches of freedom and the security of justice.[38]

The African American concern for justice also finds poetic expression in the words of Langston Hughes:

> That justice is a blind goddess
> Is a thing to which we black are wise:
> Her bandage hides two festering sores
> That once perhaps were eyes.[39]

What one sees in statements such as these is a severe criticism of an understanding of "justice" which is supportive of or indifferent to racial injustice. Hence a major characteristic of African American ethics is an ideological critique of the dominant culture's concept and practice of justice. In other words, black ethicists typically do not dwell upon the abstract question, "What is justice?" Rather, they raise more pointed questions: "*Whose* justice?" "Justice for *whom*?" "What is it about prevailing notions of justice which make them either supportive of or complacent with the existence of racial oppression?"[40]

Consequently, the language or rhetoric employed by black ethicists reflects this intense preoccupation with justice. One finds not only scholarly, rational, analytic argumentation, but also the vivid idioms and imagery characteristic of black preaching. In African American ethical discussions, one encounters not only the cool, measured discourse of the academy, but also expressions of outrage, denunciation, exhortation, lamentation, and warning characteristic of prophecy. In the words of Abraham Heshel, "The *moralists* discuss, suggest, counsel; the *prophets* proclaim, demand, insist."[41] Both genres and languages—those of the academy and those of prophecy—are found in African American religious ethics, indicative of a single-hearted concern with justice.[42]

Hence, in the African American tradition of religious ethics, one observes the primary place of justice as the central virtue and pursuit.[43] The primacy accorded to justice in no way detracts from the importance of love in the Christian ethic. Rather, the black Christian tradition insists that securing justice is an essential requirement and fundamental imperative of love.[44]

C. The Division of the Ethical Question/Task

All Americans—black and white—are morally obliged to pursue justice by working toward the creation of a racially inclusive society, free from a poisonous relationships of exploitation and privilege based on skin color. Yet while this goal is common to all, it imposes different concrete demands and imperatives depending upon whether one is in the position of systemic detriment or systemic advantage. In other words, those events and processes which are necessary to bring about a just social order (e.g., the redistribution of political power, social burdens, and access to essential human goods) will be experienced differently by the two principal racial groups—and also will impose differing ethical demands or moral obligations.

Thus the African American ethical tradition posits a division of the ethical question. In a sense, blacks and whites do not have the same ethical tasks relative to the pursuit of a racially just society. The thought of Major J. Jones is instructive here. Jones argues that the descendants of slaves and the descendants of slave owners are both bound by the Christian mandate of love, and that this requires the members of each group to contribute to the abolition of the oppressed-oppressor relationship. But the differences between the two social locations imply correspondingly different responses:

> When one talks of the liberation of black people or of the changes needed to bring about social justice, the meaning is different for each individual. For the socially advantaged white person, it means yielding old privileges, accepting new risks, and giving up traditional positions of economic advantage. For the socially disadvantaged black [person],

it means accepting a new social status, assuming new positions of power and responsibility, and acquiring a new sense of justice for those whom he had displaced as oppressors. As a black person who was once oppressed, he would now have to deal with his newly acquired powers. He would now have to determine whether he would use his newly acquired powers to empower others or to suppress them.[45]

Hence, Jones concludes that the ethical question of "What am I to do?" needs to be divided; despite the common imperative to dismantle the edifice of racial oppression, the ethical question can be answered concretely only from within a specific—a black or white—social location.

Two examples will clarify this point. On the one hand, the womanist essayist bell hooks writes that one of the most insidious effects of racial oppression is that its victims, "bombarded by messages that we have no value [and] are worthless," internalize this racism and deny their own worth, beauty, and intelligence. Hence, she posits that, for African Americans, celebrating and affirming blackness is an essential and indeed revolutionary step toward abolishing the structure of white supremacy: "Loving blackness as political resistance transforms our ways of looking and being, and thus creates the conditions necessary for us to move against the forces of domination and death and reclaim black life."[46]

On the other hand, Walt Harrington, a white man married to a black woman and the father of two interracial children, was shocked into an awareness of the depth of racism through a casual racist joke uttered in his presence. Moved by this incident, he undertook a year-long journey to discover "Black America." At the end of his journey, he writes:

But what I discovered while sitting in the dentist's chair more than a year ago, what I learned from the dentist who stopped by and casually told a racist joke about a black man who was stupid, still remains the greatest insight I have to share: *The idiot was talking about my kids!* ...

This kind of understanding changes everything. Only when I *became* black by proxy—through my son, through my daughter—could I see the racism I have been willing to tolerate. Becoming black, even for a fraction of an instant, created an urgency for justice that I couldn't feel as a white man, no matter how good-hearted. It is absolute proof of our continued racism that no white person in his or her right mind would yet volunteer to trade places, become black, in America today.[47]

Thus for white Americans, a break from one's social location of privilege is an essential step in achieving racial justice and fulfilling the Christian mandate of love.[48]

To conclude: African American religious ethics posits that the ethical questions faced by black and white Americans are not necessarily the same. A common ethical mandate—the abolition of personal and institutional racism—imposes concrete tasks and demands which differ with regard to social location. This is an insight not commonly acknowledged by most Christian ethicists.[49] In the words of Peter Paris:

> [B]lack churches faithful to the norm of the black Christian tradition have no radical doctrine of sin that readily implicates all people (white and black) in the same way. Rather, the thought of the black churches distinguishes the "sins" of black people from the "sin" of white racism, which is considered by far the most wretched.[50]

D. The Normative Vision (Eschatological Hope)

A final feature of African American religious ethics to be considered is that it is an ethic of hope. Hope is an essential requirement for an oppressed people yearning and striving for justice. Thus black religious ethics must be guided by a vision capable of inspiring and instilling that hope which can motivate and sustain a people in the face of the difficult, persistent, often elusive and perhaps permanent quest for freedom, justice, and equality—for full recognition as human beings.

African American ethicists usually articulate this hope in biblical images and metaphors. James Cone relates that in the black spirituals, "heaven" is an image used to express this guiding and sustaining hope in the midst of a hostile social milieu:

> In the black spirituals, the image of heaven served functionally to liberate the black mind from the existing values of white society, enabling black slaves to think their own thoughts and do their own things. For Tubman and Douglass, heaven meant the risk of escape to the North and Canada; for Nat Turner, it was a vision from above that broke into the minds of believers, giving them the courage and the power to take up arms against slave masters and mistresses. And for others, heaven was a perspective on the present, a spiritual, a song about "another world...not made with hands"...[enabling blacks] to transcend the enslavement of the present and to live as if the future had already come.[51]

Put another way, "heaven" offered a vision of a future social order which inspired and guided revolutionary reflection and action with regard to the already existing social arrangement. Far from being illusory, escapist, or otherworldly, "heaven" is an example of utopian thinking characterized by a profound concern with and anchoring in the present—indeed by a *subversive* relationship with regard to present historical reality. As Cone observes:

> Hope, in the black spirituals, is not a denial of history. Black hope accepts history, but believes that the historical is in motion, moving toward a divine fulfillment. *It is the belief that things can be radically otherwise than they are*: that reality is not fixed, but moving in the direction of human liberation.[52]

This writer proposes that the image of "Pentecost" can serve as a vehicle for conveying a vision of hope capable of guiding and sustaining reflection and action toward the goal of a racially just and inclusive society. In the Pentecost narrative, all the peoples of the earth heard the Good News preached in their own tongues. Viewed from this perspective, "Pentecost" becomes a metaphor for cultural pluralism and diversity, the divine grounding for the acceptance of differences among peoples and the equality of races. It becomes the religious basis for moving toward a pluralistic solution to the question of racial justice, a solution which envisions full participation and inclusion combined with a respect for cultural identity.[53] Thus "Pentecost" can serve as a biblical image of hope, sustaining ethical reflection and action which both critiques the present and strives to create a new social order: a society governed by the canons of neither "integration," nor "assimilation," nor "separation," but rather those of "transformation," the affirmation of difference, and the embrace of plural models of what is accepted as "American"—or indeed "human."[54]

III. Convergence with Roman Catholic Ethics

Earlier it was demonstrated how American Catholic moralists evidenced little interest in or sensitivity to the African American experience, especially that of racial injustice. Are we to conclude, then, that there is no possible entree in Catholic moral theology to the insights and contributions of African American religious ethics? I now offer

different points of origin-different starting points give us different ethical tasks at least two "windows" in Catholic moral reflection which can be avenues for fruitful dialogue.

A. The Recognition of Social Sin

The concept of social sin—that is, the recognition of the social consequences and embodiments of sin in public life and institutions— is one of recent and increasing importance in Catholic moral reflection. While the implications of this understanding of human sinfulness are still a subject of intense theological reflection and interest,[55] the basic premise is beyond dispute and has been endorsed by the Catholic Magisterium.[56]

The idea that sin is not merely an interior, private state of estrangement between individuals and God provides a fruitful avenue for dialogue between Catholic moral theology and the African American experience. For black Americans commonly acknowledge that not every individual white person is personally guilty of or responsible for racism; yet they are virtually unanimous in their belief that it is "whites" as a collectivity, (also known as, "the System" or "the Man") which is the real obstacle which must be overcome and transformed in their quest for racial justice.[57] Recent discussions of social sin in the Catholic tradition which highlight both the voluntary and the nonvoluntary dimensions of structural sinfulness,[58] along with the inappropriateness of "blame" while insisting upon the need for "accountability" for systemic evils,[59] are possible channels by which a conversation can occur between Catholic moralists and African American ethicists.

B. Solidarity with the Poor

Another recent and ever more important theme in Catholic ethical reflection and teaching is the concept of a moral obligation to be in solidarity with the poor. While this idea is officially accepted by the Catholic Magisterium[60] and widely used by Catholic theologians,[61] its exact meaning is somewhat imprecise and not yet the object of universal consensus. "Solidarity with the poor" refers to a faith-inspired and motivated commitment to identify oneself with the plight of the neglected, despised and insignificant of society and a consequent resolution to advocate on their behalf for a more just social order. It entails a decision to view social reality from the perspective of the victims of injustice. The U.S. bishops express this understanding of solidarity when they maintain that economic policies and decisions "must be judged in light of what they do *for* the poor, what they do *to* the poor, and what they enable the poor to do *for themselves.*"[62]

Such a stance of solidarity with the unwanted and disdained of a society promises to be a fertile common ground for the African American experience and Catholic moral theology. For a committed stance of solidarity entails a change of one's social location—a social conversion—on the part of the privileged.[63] This notion of solidarity is very congenial with the division of the ethical task posited by African American ethicists. The insights of African American ethicists could help make more concrete who are the poor that Catholics are called to be in solidarity with in North America. In U.S. society the poor are disproportionately people of color victimized by the double oppression of race and class; thus an existential appreciation and appropriation on the part of Catholic ethicists of the implications of a stance of solidarity with the poor should logically lead to a greater awareness of and receptivity to the African American experience.

Conclusion

"Will the Church of tomorrow solve the problem of the Color Line?" So asked the great essayist, W.E.B. Du Bois, in 1931. His answer, to put it mildly, was grim: "[T]he Christian church will do nothing conclusive or effective; it will not settle these problems; on the contrary it will as long as possible and whenever possible avoid them; in this, as in nearly every great modern moral controversy, it will be found consistently on the wrong side...."[64] These are indeed sobering words. I hesitate to take exception to the insight and wisdom of someone of the stature of Du Bois. Perhaps it is evidence of the optimism of youth, hopefully it is a sign of a trust in the Spirit who descended at Pentecost. In any event, this essay is an act of hope that the American Catholic moral community not only can be, but will be, enriched by the insights of its fellow believers and citizens of African descent, so that one day it will be true that the African American experience and U.S. Catholic moral theology are "strangers and aliens no longer."

Notes

[1] Immanuel Kant, *Critique of Pure Reason* (New York: St. Martin's Press, 1965) 635.

[2] My phrasing of these questions is indebted to Richard M. Gula, *Reason Informed by Faith: Foundations of Catholic Morality* (Mahwah, NJ: Paulist Press, 1989) 7 and 8.

[3] James H. Cone, *The Spirituals and the Blues: An Interpretation* (New York: Seabury Press, 1972) 72.

[4] In defining racism in terms of a systemic distribution and defense of racially conferred (or denied) privileges, I have been influenced by the following: Peggy McIntosh, "White Privilege and Male Privilege: A Personal Account of Coming to See Correspondences through Work in Women's Studies" (Wellesley College Center for Research on Women, 1988); David T. Wellman, *Portraits of White Racism,* 2nd Edition (New York: Cambridge University Press, 1993); Ruth Frankenberg, *The Social Construction of Whiteness: White Women, Race Matters* (Minneapolis: University of Minnesota Press, 1993); and Joe R. Feagin and Hernan Vera, *White Racism: The Basics* (New York: Routledge, 1995). Thus "racism" connotes a network of unearned and unmerited privileges, advantages, and benefits conferred to some and denied to others because of racial differences—and—a complex of beliefs, rationalizations, and practices used to justify, explain, and defend this network of unearned advantage and privilege.

[5] Jamie T. Phelps, "The Sources of Theology: African-American Catholic Experience in the United States." Unpublished paper read at the Catholic Theological Society of America, June 1988, Toronto, Canada.

[6] A similar point of view is expressed by the African American ethicist Theodore Walker, in his *Empower the People. Social Ethics for the African-American Church* (Maryknoll, NY: Orbis Books, 1991) 3.

[7] U.S. National Advisory Commission on Civil Disorders, *Report of the National Advisory Commission on Civil Disorders* (New York: Bantam Books, 1968) 10.

[8] Robert H. Springer, "Notes on Moral Theology: July 1969-March 1970," *Theological Studies* 31 (1970) 509.

[9] This silence or neglect is all the more disconcerting when one considers that from 1965 until recently, the "Notes" were authored by Richard A. McCormick, who is arguably the most eminent and respected authority in the American Catholic moral academy. I hasten to add that this observation is not meant to denigrate McCormick's valuable contributions to the discipline of moral theology, or more importantly, to suggest that he is in some way unique with regard to the lack of attention given to matters of race. The same phenomena of silence and/or cursory treatment also are evidenced in the works of Germain Grisez and Charles E. Curran, two other influential American Catholic ethicists. As this essay

will demonstrate, McCormick's silence on racial justice typifies the stance of American Catholic ethicists in general.

[10]Gerald Kelly, "Notes on Moral Theology, 1946," *Theological Studies* 8 (1947) 112-14.

[11]In addition to the article cited, discussions of racial justice can be found in Theological Studies (TS) as follows: G. Kelly, "Notes on Moral Theology, 1951," TS 13 (1952) 67-70; G. Kelly, "Notes on Moral Theology, 1952," TS 14 (1953) 50; G. Kelly and John C. Ford, "Notes on Moral Theology, 1953," TS 15 (1954) 80-82; John R. Connery, "Notes on Moral Theology," TS 17 (1956) 568-69; John J. Lynch, "Notes on Moral Theology," TS 18 (1957) 221-23; Joseph J. Farraher, TS 24 (1963) 92-94: and G. Kelly. "Notes on Moral Theology," TS 24 (1963) 649-51.

[12]One should note, however, that Kelly does discuss the possibility of there being morally acceptable forms of segregation—that is, "segregation by mutual agreement and with equal rights." While such racial separation would be a "tragedy," he concludes that it "might be tolerated as the lesser of two evils" if it proved impossible for the races to live together peacefully. Cf. "Notes on Moral Theology, 1951," TS 13 (1952) 68.

[13]It is only in 1963 that one finds an unequivocal moral condemnation of racial discrimination as a violation of "justice"—and this in the context of viewing the promotion of racial justice as an essential tool in the fight against communism. One is left with the definite impression that the pursuit of racial justice is not viewed as a worthy end in itself. Cf. J. Farraher, "Notes on Moral Theology," TS 24 (1963) 92.

[14]J. Lynch, "Notes on Moral Theology," TS 18 (1957) 222.

[15]Francis J. Gilligan, "Moral Aspects of Segregation in Education," *Catholic Theological Society of America Proceedings* 13 (1958) 51-60 (with a summary of the subsequent discussion from 60-62); and Joseph T. Leonard, "Current Theological Questions in Racial Relations," *Catholic Theological Society of America Proceedings* 19 (1964) 81-91.

[16]An examination of the minutes of the Society's gatherings published in the *Proceedings* reveals that several attempts were made to have the issue of racial justice considered by the body before 1958, but to no avail. In 1954, one finds the topic "Morality of Resistance Movements" proposed, yet it was dropped (cf. "Report of the Committee on Current Problems," *Proceedings* 9 [1954] 236). In 1956, the topic "Moral Aspects of the Movement toward Racial Integration" was proposed for the Society's consideration that year, but was passed over in favor of lectures on "The Concept of Servile Work," "Suitable Penances for Different Classes of Penitents," and "Habitual Sin" ("Report of the Committee on Current Problems," *Proceedings* 11 [1956] 262). In 1957, the topic "Moral Aspects of the Movement toward Racial Integration" was passed over once again in favor of presentations on "The Morality of Situation Ethics," "The Changing Concept of Servile Work," and "The Morality of Right-to-Work Laws" ("Report of the Committee on Current Problems," *Pro-*

ceedings 12 [1957] 242). One gains from this history an appreciation for the priorities of the moralists of that time.

[17]Gilligan, "Moral Aspects of Segregation in Education," 54-55.

[18]Gilligan, "Moral Aspects of Segregation in Education," 56. Note again how the fear of Communism, or more accurately, the fear that the Communists would exploit American racial injustices to their benefit, was key for motivating people to be concerned about racism. The struggle against racism was often not seen as a worthy goal in itself.

[19]C. Luke Salm, "Moral Aspects of Segregation in Education—Digest of the Discussion," 61; emphasis in the original.

[20]Leonard, "Current Theological Questions in Race Relations," 82.

[21]Leonard, "Current Theological Questions in Race Relations," 83

[22]Joseph R. Nearon, "Preliminary Report: Research Committee for Black Theology," *Proceedings of the Catholic Theological Society of America* 29 (1974) 413-17. By way of comparison, note that the first woman (Agnes Cunningham) addressed the Society in 1969.

[23]Nearon, "Research Committee for Black Theology," 414-15.

[24]David Hollenbach, "Seminar on Moral Theology: The Future Agenda of Catholic Moral Theology in America," *Proceedings* 37 (1982) 176-177.

[25]John La Farge, *The Catholic Viewpoint on Race Relations* (Garden City, NY: Hanover House, 1956); Joseph T. Leonard, *Theology and Race Relations* (Milwaukee, WI: Bruce Publishing, 1963); Daniel C. Maguire, *A New American Justice* (Minneapolis, MN: Winston Press, 1980; reissued as *A Case for Affirmative Action* (Dubuque, IA: Shepherd Inc., 1992). In this connection, we should also take note of Christopher F. Mooney, *Inequality and the American Conscience* (Mahwah, NJ: Paulist Press, 1982).

[26]National Conference of Catholic Bishops, Brothers and Sisters to Us (Washington, DC: United States Catholic Conference, 1979). One should also be aware of two previous statements by the U.S. bishops on race matters: *Discrimination and the Christian Conscience* (1958) and *The National Race Crisis* (1968). It should also be noted that none of these statements has received significant scholarly attention or pastoral implementation. On this point, cf. the statement of the U.S. Bishops' Committee on Black Catholics, *For the Love of One Another: A Special Message on the Occasion of the Tenth Anniversary of Brothers and Sisters to Us* (1989).

[27]This despite Gerald Kelly's realization in 1963 that "a moral theology course, at least in this country, would be unrealistic and basically defective if it included no special treatment of race relations" ("Notes on Moral Theology," *Theological Studies* 24 [1963] 650; emphasis added).

[28]One should note that we will not be concerned with the whole range and corpus of Black Theology, but only with specifically ethical concerns.

[29]Peter J. Paris, *The Social Teaching of the Black Churches* (Philadelphia: Fortress Press, 1985) 10, 14; emphasis added.

[30]Paris, *Social Teaching of Black Churches*, 11.

[31]Paris, *Social Teaching of Black Churches*, 14.

[32]Preston N. Williams, "Afro-American Religious Ethics," in James F. Childress and John Macquarrie (eds.), *The Westminster Dictionary of Christian Ethics* (Philadelphia: Westminster Press, 1986) 12.

[33]William M. Finnin, Jr., "Ethics of Universal Wholeness: An Assessment of the Work of Preston N. Williams," *The Iliff Review* 36 (Spring 1979) 28; citing Williams, "Criteria for Decision-Making for Social Ethics in the Black Community," *Journal of the Interdenominational Center* I (Fall 1973) 67; emphasis added.

[34]Cornel West, "Black Leadership and the Pitfalls of Racial Reasoning," in Toni Morrison (ed.), *Race-ing Justice, En-gendering Power: Essays on Anita Hill, Clarence Thomas, and the Construction of Social Reality* (New York: Pantheon Books. 1992) 390-401.

[35]Cf. Enoch Oglesby, who examines King's commitment to the "beloved community" and concludes that the formation of an inclusive community is the "intentional focus" of the Black Church's socio-ethical reflection (in his *Ethics and Theology from the Other Side: Sounds of Moral Struggle* [Lanham, MD: University Press of America, 1979] 146).

[36]Paris, *Social Teaching of the Black Churches*, 10, 11.

[37]Bishop C. M. Tanner (1900), cited by Paris, *Social Teaching of the Black Churches,* 19-20.

[38]Martin Luther King, Jr., *A Testament of Hope: The Essential Writings of Martin Luther King, Jr.* (edited by James Melvin Washington), (San Francisco: Harper and Row, 1986) 217.

[39]Langston Hughes, "Justice," in Dudley Randall (ed.), *The Black Poets* (New York: Bantam Books, 1971) 87.

[40]On this point, see Robert Michael Franklin, "In Pursuit of Justice: Martin Luther King, Jr., and John Rawls," *Journal of Religious Ethics* 18 (Fall 1990) 5777; and David W. Wills, "Racial Justice and the Limit of American Liberalism," *Journal of Religious Ethics* 6 (Fall 1978) 187-200.

[41]Abraham J. Heschel, *The Prophets,* Volume I (New York: Harper and Row, 1962) 215.

[42]Theodore Walker, Jr., *Empower the People: Social Ethics for the African-American Church* (Maryknoll, NY: Orbis Books, 1991) 13-14.

[43]Peter J. Paris, "The Character of Liberation Ethics," in Lorine M. Getz and Ruy O. Costa (eds.), *Struggles for Solidarity: Liberation Theologies in Tension* (Minneapolis, MN: Fortress Press, 1992) 139.

[44]For example, Enoch H. Oglesby, an African-American Christian ethicist, criticizes what he calls an "*over-commitment* to the principle of love as the paradigm of the moral life—especially in light of the realities of oppression and suffering in modern society." While not denying the centrality of love in the ethic of Jesus, Oglesby argues that "there is far too little attention given to the idea of justice as a requirement of love, particularly in regard to the black man's struggle for status, social responsibility, equality, and full personhood in the American cultural system." In contradistinction to this position, Oglesby argues that the Chris-

tian ethic, "radically conceived," would show that "justice is not only a requisite for human community, but a fundamental ethical imperative of love." Thus Oglesby's fundamental argument: "There is an apparent over-commitment to the love principle without careful consideration of what it demands that we do in a society deeply implicated in the guilt of social injustice and racial prejudice" (*Ethics and Theology from the Other Side*, 140; emphasis in the original).

[45]Major J. Jones, *Christian Ethics for Black Theology. The Politics of Liberation* (Nashville, TN: Abingdon Press, 1974) 17-18. His discussion of this point takes place from 16-23. For Theodore Walker's appropriation of this insight, see *Empower the People*, p. 17 at note 13.

[46]bell hooks, "Loving Blackness as Political Resistance," in her *Black Looks: Race and Representation* (Boston, MA: South End Press, 1992) 19-20.

[47]Walt Harrington, *Crossings: A White Man's Journey into Black America* (New York: HarperCollins, 1992) 447.

[48]For a further discussion of this task of social conversion on the part of white Americans, see Bryan N. Massingale, "The Social Dimensions of Sin and Reconciliation in the Theologies of James H. Cone and Gustavo Gutiérrez: A Critical Comparative Examination," (S.T.D. dissertation, Rome: Academia Alphonsiana, 1991) 187-91.

[49]Jones, *Christian Ethics for Black Theology*, 16.

[50]Paris, *Social Teaching of Black Churches*, 15-16. See also Delores S. Williams, "A Womanist Perspective on Sin," in Emilie M. Townes (ed.), *A Troubling in My Soul: Womanist Perspectives on Evil and Suffering* (Maryknoll, NY: Orbis Books, 1993) 130-49.

[51]Cone, *The Spirituals and the Blues*, 95.

[52]Cone, *The Spirituals and the Blues*, 95-96; emphasis added.

[53]Paris, *Social Teaching of Black Churches*, 100-01. See also the following articulation of the ethical perspective of Preston Williams: "Human community, at its best, becomes an inclusive community, culturally pluralistic, racially diverse, richly heterogeneous. 'I demand that my history also be saved. I demand pluralistic communities and a pluralistic world.' The anthropological assumptions of Dr. Williams' social ethics are inclusive, communitarian, and pluralistic" (Finnan, "Ethics of Universal Wholeness," 23; citing Williams, "James Cone and the Problem of a Black Religious Ethic," *Harvard Theological Review* 65 [1972] 491).

[54]For a sampling of the growing literature dealing with the interests of African American ethicists in the goal of social and cultural pluralism, see: Harold Cruse, *Plural but Equal: Blacks and Minorities in America's Plural Society* (New York: Quill/William Morrow, 1987); Paris, *Social Teaching of Black Churches*; and Walker, *Empower the People*. For a discussion from the black perspective of the dangers inherent in extreme pluralism— pluralism divorced from an ethical mooring—see Cornel West, "The Traps of Tribalism," *Emerge* 4 (March 1993) 42-44.

[55]For example, see Gregory Baum, "Structures of Sin," in Gregory Baum and Robert Ellsberg (eds.), *The Logic of Solidarity* (Maryknoll, NY: Orbis

Books, 1989) 110-25; Mark O'Keefe, *What Are They Saying about Social Sin?* (Mahwah, NJ: Paulist Press, 1990); and Massingale, "The Social Dimensions of Sin and Reconciliation in the Theologies of James H. Cone and Gustavo Gutiérrez."

[56]Cf. John Paul II, *Sollicitudo Rei Socialis* (1987) #36-37.

[57]Roy Brooks contends, accurately in my judgment, that one of the essential ingredients of the African American experience is "the belief that society ('the system' or 'the Man') is more foe than friend, a theme echoed by African American writers and social activists from the days of slavery to recent times" (*Rethinking the American Race Problem* [Berkeley, CA: University of California Press, 1990] 180).

[58]See Baum, "Structures of Sin," 113-16.

[59]Massingale, "The Social Dimensions of Sin and Reconciliation," 456-460.

[60]John Paul II, *Sollicitudo Rei Socialis,* #38-40.

[61]For a popular presentation of this idea, consult Peter J. Henriot, *Opting for the Poor: A Challenge for North Americans* (Washington, DC: Center of Concern, 1990).

[62]National Conference of Catholic Bishops, *Economic Justice for All: Pastoral Letter on Catholic Social Teaching and the U.S. Economy,* #24.

[63]The thoughts of Gustavo Gutierrez are especially instructive here: "Accepting solidarity with the poor involves a conversion to the Lord as a break with what has gone before and a beginning of a new way.... Evangelical conversion (*metanoia*) means a break with our mental categories, with our social group (culture, class, race), with our affective and emotional attitudes, with our secret complicities with a world in which the poor do not occupy the place God's preferential and gratuitous love entitles them to. The social dimensions of conversion to God—of every Christian and of the whole Church—became clear from the moment we recognized that it has to go through solidarity with the poor and oppressed" (Gustavo Gutierrez, "Drink from Your Own Well," in Casiano Floristan and Christian Duquoc [eds.], *Learning to Pray. Concilium* 159 [New York: Seabury Press, 1982] 42).

[64]W.E.B. Du Bois, "Will the Church Remove the Color Line? (1931)," in Andrew Paschal (ed.), *A W.E.B. Du Bois Reader* (New York: Collier Books Macmillan Publishing, 1971) 264-66.

Response to Bryan Massingale

Paul Wadell, C.P., Ph.D.
Catholic Theological Union: Chicago, Illinois

Introduction

I first want to say how happy I am to have the opportunity to respond to Bryan's paper. It is not always the case that reading something in ethics excites me, but reading Bryan's superb essay certainly did. One of the things that impressed me most about his paper is that it was written with tremendous passion and conviction and heart, something I think ought to characterize contemporary Christian ethics more often.

I wish to focus my response first on Bryan's pivotal and unquestionable contention that American Catholic ethics has given scant attention to the moral problem of racism—what Bryan rightly calls a "pattern of omission and neglect"—and suggest three reasons why I think this might be the case. Secondly, I want to look briefly at three of the four characteristics of African American Religious Ethics he underscores and reflect on how they night challenge the prevailing methodology in U.S. Catholic moral theology.

Why Racism Has Been a
Neglected Topic in U.S. Roman Catholic Ethics

What then about Bryan's charge that there has been no significant interest by American Catholic ethics in what is arguably the most persistent and insidious human rights issue in America. I think there are three reasons for this. First, there is a problem with the prevailing methodology in Roman Catholic ethics today. It is characterized by the conviction that Christian ethics and human ethics are basically the same. The intent is to show that Christian ethics is authentically human and of universal significance, but the result too often is first to collapse the Christian into abstract and unhistorical understandings of humanity so that our concrete convictions as believers have relatively no impact on our moral thinking; and, secondly, to be so concerned about the universality of our moral theology that we lose all sight of the concrete and particular; in short, a modern liberal understanding of the human both governs and limits our understanding of ourselves as Christian.

As Bryan says at the outset of his paper, the central question of ethics for Christians is "What manner of living is congruent with belief in the God of Jesus Christ?" This question seldom gets asked in contemporary Catholic ethics because it is too quickly presumed that being Christian adds nothing of normative significance to what it means to be human and it is judged too specific to matter to people who are not Christian. One ironic result of this is that the central Christian virtues of charity and justice collapse into that most modern of virtues, namely, being nice to one another but by and large leaving each other alone.

Similarly, the overriding desire in Catholic ethics to have a universal morality that can say something to everybody tends to ignore or minimize the extreme importance of culture, history, and social environment not only in shaping our understanding of the good, but also in conditioning our ability even to see the good and know when it is being violated. As Bryan suggests in his paper, if Christian ethics is too easily swallowed up in a very general, abstract, and unhistorical understanding of humanity, it lacks the appreciation for concreteness and particularity necessary to see the problem of racism and recognize it as a sin of injustice. In short, contemporary American Catholic ethics does a good job of seeing humanity but a poor job of seeing individuals, and as long as this is the case it will be slow in responding to victims of injustice or people who suffer.

A second reason I think American Catholic ethics has ignored the sin of racism is that its dominant methodology is bereft of hospitality. This is captured in Bryan's comment that few Catholic ethicists have even asked about an African-American's experience of reality, much less been concerned about it. The fact that in 1982 racism was not even mentioned as a noteworthy moral issue shows that most Catholic ethicists think everything is okay. This is a glaring lack of hospitality.

Hospitality in this sense is not a matter of etiquette but a prerequisite of justice. It means something as simple yet challenging as asking a victim of racism, "Well, how are things with you?"

That few American Catholic moralists have posed this question to African-Americans is telling and until we do so our moral reasoning not only will be extremely narrow and provincial, and thus incapable of justice, but will also be little more than an enlightened self-interest that we have identified as moral and good. As Thomas Ogletree stresses in his book *Hospitality to the Stranger,* those in positions of power and influence need those who have suffered from injustice to show us the limitations, bias, and self-deception that creeps into so much that we take for granted. This is why he says ethics must begin in an experience of de-centering when an encounter with one who suffers challenges us to rethink what we for too long have taken for granted. Hospitality is a precondition for justice and justice is a precondition for morality. As Bryan's paper suggests, American Catholic ethics can move to justice when it begins showing hospitality to the stories, experiences, and challenges of African-Americans.

Third, American Catholic ethics has neglected the African American experience because it is marked by too much fantasy and not enough reverence and repentance. Usually we think of fantasy as something exciting and uplifting, or at least something innocent, but I am using it in the somber sense of the moral philosopher Iris Murdoch who defines it as a distortion of moral vision based on a chronic misreading of the world or other people precisely because to see them truthfully would challenge us to conversion. This is what is at work in the fact, as Bryan stressed, that so often in moral discourse African Americans are "treated as objects of white study, analysis, and charity, but rarely seen as subjects capable of independent action or reflection; as he put it, "there is no acknowledgment of a sense of black agency."

The problem with fantasy is that if our vision is not truthful, neither will our actions be truthful. Our behavior reflects our perceptions. If I see any human being not as subject but as object, I cannot possibly treat him or her justly. Without truthful vision there cannot be genuine virtue; thus, the vice of fantasy must be overcome by the virtues of repentance and reverence because both enable us to appreciate every human being as a person due justice and respect.

African American Religious Ethics
As Challenge to Roman Catholic Ethics

What about the three characteristics of African American Religious Ethics outlined by Bryan? How do they challenge the prevailing methodology in Roman Catholic ethics today? Bryan spoke first of the strong African American conviction of the kinship and equality of all persons under God, emphasizing that for African Americans this "is not an abstract idea but a 'normative condition.'" This reminds us that the central task of Christian ethics is not guiding the autonomous individual to good decisions of conscience, but the establishing of a community of justice and peace through reconciliation. In his book *The Making of Moral Theology,* John Mahoney describes this as an "ethics of koinonia," stressing that community is not a sideline of Christian ethics, but its heart and soul because God wants us to be one. Thus, one implication of Bryan's analysis is that the moral mission of the Church is to witness in its own life and to the world the community of justice and peace to which God calls everyone; in short, the Church's moral responsibility is to be both a symbol and an agent of community. In this respect, I think Bryan's paper is calling not for a revised personal ethics and not even for a revised social ethics, but for an ecclesial ethics.

The second characteristic of African-American ethics outlined in Bryan's paper is a passionate concern for justice. As Aquinas wrote, the virtue of justice means that as we live we fulfill our obligations to everyone and harm no one. That's a daunting challenge, reminding us of the bonds we have with everyone and the responsibility we have to be attentive to their needs. As Aquinas saw it, justice was not a consequence of morality but constitutive of morality.

But if Bryan is correct that too often today our prevailing notions of justice fail those responsibilities and obligations because they either blind us to the existence of racism or actually support it, then the only way the centrality of justice can be assured in Christian ethics is if we begin ethical reflection not with general reflections about what it means to be human, but with the cries of the people who are told they are expendable. The weak, helpless, and downtrodden, the countless victims of racism, must be at the center of our ethical reflection, not on the fringe. Ethics must begin with the concrete and particular, but specifically with concrete, particular cases of injustice. Racism cannot be bracketed while we consider other dimensions of the moral life, but must be its starting point. There is no way I can proceed to talk about what a genuinely human life is or what it means to be moral and good until I reckon with the crimes of racism.

Finally, what about hope? It is here, I think, that African American ethics can make its most radical and urgent contribution to American Catholic ethics. Oddly enough, while Catholic ethics is characterized by optimism, there is a strange absence of hope. The two are not the same. As Bryan suggests, hope is impossible without a "sustaining and nourishing vision" of magnanimous possibilities, heroic and noble possibilities truly worthy of ourselves. For the most part, American Catholic ethics lacks a vision capable of truly inspiring and motivating people to what is best because it has a hard time suggesting any worthy objects of hope. Put differently, what we hope for is so impoverished because it is little more than a reflection of the puny hopes of our dominant society.

Quoting James Cone, Bryan mentioned that the black spirituals functioned to liberate African Americans from the existing values of white society. In order to hope again, perhaps white society needs to be liberated from some existing values as well, particularly materialism, consumerism, and individualism. Again quoting Cone, Bryan stressed that hope for African Americans has always been sustained by the belief that things could be radically other than they are. If white Americans are to find again a deep and compelling sense of hope, they need to see that keeping things as they are isn't too promising for any of us. In this respect, perhaps the greatest contribution of Bryan's paper is to remind us that a commitment to justice and a conversion from racism frees all of us for genuine hope.

Conclusion

In conclusion, by focusing on the sin of racism, Bryan challenges American Catholic moral theology to a thorough restructuring. It is important to understand that he is calling us to something very different. Bryan's paper answers the challenge of Vatican II to rethink Catholic moral theology entirely. What he summons us to is a revised moral theology marked by hospitality, reverence, and repentance. It would be a moral theology rooted in the concrete and particular and one in which the central confession of our faith, namely that Jesus is Lord for us, would be pivotal. Finally, it would be a moral theology centered in justice and seeking community, a moral theology that saw its task to be fashioning communities of reconciliation and peace. In this respect, the model Bryan proposes provides an answer to the central question of Christian ethics: "What manner of living is congruent with belief in the God of Jesus Christ?" To wrestle with that question ought to be liberating for all of us.

Foundations for Catholic Theology in an African American Context

M. Shawn Copeland, Ph.D.

Marquette University: Milwaukee, Wisconsin

An ethics of historical responsibility for thought, truth, and belief commands us to subject to discussion, and to the judgment of our experience, what the dominator's *activism of the offerer*, of importunity, does not cease imperiously to propose to us…. [W]e have to demand of the Christianity soliciting us that it enter into the framework of our movement for liberty in its most concrete expressions, and that it take the form…of self-determination rediscovered and rectified.[1]

Introduction

In his methodological writings, Bernard Lonergan mapped the issues to be met, the choices to be made in theology's new context: the rise of historical-mindedness and its challenge to a classicist world-view; the breakdown of the classical mediation of meaning and the emergence of a modern mediation; the precarious transition from a classicist notion to an empirical notion of culture; the challenges stemming from the new human sciences, from the problems of hermeneutics and critical history.[2] On Lonergan's account, if these exigencies are to be met adequately in both the theoretical and pastoral contexts,[3] Catholic theology must undergo a "total transformation," a "complete restructuring."[4] Moreover, on Lonergan's account, such a renewed theology requires "a new type of foundations," rooted in intellectual, religious, and moral conversion: a cognitive foundation at once empirical, critical, methodical, dialectical, and normative; a religious foundation at once historical and communal, yet personally experienced in the mystery of falling-in-love with God, realized in lived transvaluation of values, and grounding theological practice.[5] Observing that "a theology is the product not only of a faith but also of a culture,"[6] Lonergan challenges the Catholic theologian to acknowledge, not only "a multiplicity of cultural traditions," but "the possibility of diverse differentiations of human consciousness" within those traditions. The upshot of this for the future of Catholic Christian faith is that there will be—indeed, must be—a "multiplicity of theologies" that express that one, same faith.[7] This is an effort toward meeting my obligation to contribute to that reorientation and that future.

My topic is quite subtle. To put it starkly: *What are the foundations for a Catholic theology in an African American historical, cultural, and social (i.e., political, economic, technological) context? Are there African American intellectual and cultural resources capable of funding an authentically Catholic theology? What are those African American intellectual and cultural resources? And, finally, what might an African American Catholic theology look like?* For the sake of convenience, these questions will be treated in three sections. The first section addresses notions of perspective, conversion, and foundations in and for theology. For the most part, my presentation is compatible with Lonergan's, but there are some differences, particularly in the discussion of religious conversion and in the inclusion of Robert Doran's notion of psychic conversion. Relating Lonergan's work to depth psychology, Doran situates psychic conversion in the context of the notion of self-appropriation and brings out the implications of the concrete embodiment of intentionality. This dimension of conversion has a real and crucial relevance for the African American theologian. The second and lengthiest section is recursive and archaeological:[8] returning, excavating, reconstructing *base-line religious consciousness*. Spiraling out of religious experience and conversion, that consciousness is characterized by critical and mystical apprehension of forms of the sacred and by the blending and fusing of fragments of traditional West African religio-cultural ritual, orientation, self-understanding, aesthetic-moral meanings and values. Moreover, that consciousness arranges and orders itself as desire and ecstasy, prayer and song, vision and possession, shout and dance, the solemnity and joy of 'black religion.' Drawing from this recursive inquiry, the *third section* presents some marks or features of a theological mediation 'authentically Black and truly Catholic.'

Section One: Conversion, Foundations, Perspective

Lonergan's account of method in theology is provocative as it envisions theology as a set of related and recurrent operations cumulatively advancing towards understanding.[9] To that end, Lonergan conceives of and distinguishes eight distinct tasks in theology: research, interpretation, history, dialectic, foundations, doctrines, systematics, and communications. The first four of these tasks constitute *mediating theology*. Through attentive, intelligent, reasonable, responsible exercise of the functions of research, interpretation, history, dialectic, the theologian critically appropriates the past, and is formed in encounter with and by her or his religious tradition as well as the cultural and historical context(s) of that tradition.[10] The second four specialties constitute *mediated theology*. Through responsible, reasonable, intelligent, and attentive exercise of the specialties of foundations, doctrines, systematics, and communications, the theologian confronts problems or questions that permeate her or his own cultural context and moves to theological understanding and creative communication continuous with authentic religious tradition, faithful to the canons of intellectual probity, relevant to the believing community, cognizant of the culture. These two phases of theology dynamically interact with one another, especially through *dialectic* and the conversion it promotes—crucial moments of personal decision, evaluation and choice.

Most properly, *foundations* concerns mediated theology and is rooted in dialectic and the conversions it promotes. Dialectic is a critical specialization of theological intelligence: it identifies, compares, and evaluates conflicting accounts of the past, different interpretations of the same events, opposing interests and emphases of researchers. Moreover, dialectic is concerned, not only with intellectual hermeneutics, but also with "evaluative hermeneutics."[11] To what has been attained in research, interpretation, and history is added an evaluative history and interpretation. The theologian evaluates, for example, the differences and the *implications* of those differences in the accounts of "slave culture" put forward by Sterling Stuckey, Abram Kardiner and Lionel Ovesey, and Lawrence Levine; in the studies of religious practices among the enslaved peoples in the ante-bellum period by Mechal Sobel and Albert Raboteau; in the histories recounted by Gayraud Wilmore and Cyprian Davis.[12]

As evaluative, dialectic uncovers differences, whether these are irreducible, complementary, or genetic; as critique, dialectic demonstrates whether these differences are rooted in misunderstanding, in the absence of new data, in *biased* presuppositions or willful rejection and/or exclusion of new information or insight.[13] Still, it is the theologian who evaluates and the ground of that evaluation is given in the criteria of her or his own consciousness. If the theologian adheres to these criteria attentively, intelligently, reasonably, and responsibly, then she or he is lead to true judgments of fact and of value.

In the mediating phase of theology, the African American theologian, not only critically engages and appropriates the historical, cultural, religious past of Africans enslaved in the United States, but is *formed* by that engagement. For in this phase of theology, the theologian encounters persons and this encounter is not an "optional addition to interpretation and to history."[14] The African American Catholic theologian, then, has a responsibility to encounter the community of the historic dead, those children, women, and men who were the concrete human sacrifice of the Middle Passage and its slave-legacy. An encounter with our historic dead calls for critical humble understanding of the compound and complex religious, cultural, and historical warp and weft of their structured oppression; appreciation of their toughness of heart and spirit, their values and creativity; criticism of their defects, esteem for their excellences; witness to their defiance, failure, and triumph. This encounter calls for more: African American theologians must allow their living to be challenged by the "maldistribution, negative quality, enormity, and transgenerational character" of the suffering of the enslaved peoples;[15] must open their hearts, minds, and lives to be challenged at their roots by the words and deeds of the enslaved peoples; must embrace and be embraced by their hope; must honor their struggle. Again: this encounter is not an optional addition to interpretation and to history. The theologians' interpretation depends upon their own self-understandings; the history they write depends upon their horizons. In the fateful, humbling encounter with our historic dead, the theologians' self-understandings and horizons are put to the test.

If African American Catholics are to elaborate a theology, authentically Black and truly Catholic, that elaboration implies a distinctive *perspective.* The term perspective connotes the religious, moral, intellectual, and psychic outcome of rigorous research, interpretation, history, and dialectic; a particular accumulation and consolidation of experience, insight, understanding, and judgment; of reflection, choice, decision, and action; of image, metaphor, symbol, and representation. Perspective, then, is an achievement; it is the accumulation and consolidation of insights and developments, not only in scholarship, but also in self-understanding. The *conversion* dialectic promotes results in the transformation of the subject and the subject's world. Conversion here adverts to a fourfold movement: religious, moral, and intellectual, and psychic; each is a different type of event yet, each is related to the others.[16] With the term *foundations*, I mean to connote the living and lived decision of religious, moral, intellectual, and psychic conversion.

Religious experience is "that mode of experience [in] which [a woman or a man] apprehends and discovers the sacredness of the forms of the world."[17] In this mode, a woman or a man seeks, grasps, and loves transcendent reality. Given the blending, fusion, and the reconfiguration of traditional African religious symbols as well as the historic importance of Christianity for African American religious valorization and interpretation, that transcendent reality is revealed, met, and known through contact with the Hebrew and Christian Scriptures. Indeed, that transcendent reality is *identical* with the God who acts in history to manifest divine creativity and power, justice and love, wrath and mercy as witnessed by those Scriptures. Moreover, that one same God has revealed, met, known, and loved the enslaved people; and the enslaved people have met, acknowledged, confessed, known, and loved that one same God. When that God is felt or met powerfully, pervasively in prayer, in vision, in shout, in ecstatic dance, the power and dynamism of that love redirects a woman's or a man's life. The power and dynamism of that love transforms, grounds, and governs all her or his decisions, choices, and actions.

Religious conversion, then, denotes a turning in love toward God, a decision or choice for God. It is a transforming experience of divine grace. Religious conversion may be dramatic, overwhelming, abrupt. Here is an excerpt from a freed woman's narrative of conversion:

> When God struck me dead with His power...I was in my house alone and I declare unto you when His power struck me I died.... In my vision I saw hell and the devil. I was crawling along a high brick wall, it seems, and it looked like I would fall into a dark roaring pit. I looked away to the east and saw Jesus. He called to me and said, "Arise and follow me."[18]

Yet, religious conversion need not be so dramatic; it is, after all, a "natural phenomenon that may take as many forms as human need dictates."[19] Thus, religious conversion may be experienced as a fitful and gradual turning towards a full and complete transformation of the whole of our living and feeling, thoughts, words, and deeds.

Religious consciousness is a distinct mediation of communal and personal transformation for African Americans and that consciousness is the basis for aesthetic and moral conversion. In African American perspective, the general and primary context of *moral conversion* has been community. Kimberly Rae Connor observes: "the early African-American community possessed its own norms and ideals and forms of expression that created an environment where the emphasis was placed on cooperation, respect, and individual fulfillment through conversion within the community."[20]

Moral conversion meant that the person was centered within the community and the community was centered within the person. The community embraced the flourishing and good of the person and the person embraced the flourishing and good of the community. Despite the materially punishing isolation of *de facto* and *de jure* segregation, the African American community shaped and sustained crucial virtues: regard for the wisdom and lives of elder men and women; fortitude and resolve; truth-telling; self-respecting decorum and demeanor; communal participation in child-rearing; respect for human life, even the lives of members of the oppressing community.

Intellectual conversion is the radical clarification which overcomes the ocular epistemological illusion, so rampant in Eurocentric philosophy, according to which all knowing is looking and objectivity is seeing what is there to be seen. This illusion blurs the distinction between the world of immediacy, the sum of what is seen, heard, touched, tasted, smelt, felt, and the world mediated by meaning. Further, the metaphor of 'knowing as looking' fosters a kind of picture thinking or thinking in visual images.[21] Such a foundation for knowing is easily seduced to support the Eurocentric aesthetic 'normative gaze' with its attendant racist, sexist, imperialist, and pornographic connotations.[22] Visual images are incapable of mediating the normative and critical exigence of human intelligence and reasonableness. This illusion is dispelled by a cognitional theory based on the theologian's authentic appropriation of her or his operations of conscious intentionality. Knowing is not merely taking a look, but the dynamic conjunction of experiencing, understanding, and judging; objectivity is established not in seeing what is *already-out-there-*

now to be seen, but by the compound criteria of experiencing, understanding, judging, believing, and deciding. "The reality known is not just looked at; it is given in experience, organized and extrapolated by understanding, posited by judgment and belief."[23]

More than ninety years ago, W.E.B. DuBois eloquently and poignantly articulated the issue of psychic conversion in the context of the condition of African Americans:

> [t]he Negro is a sort of seventh son [*sic*], born with a veil, and gifted with second-sight in this American world—a world which yields him [*sic*] no true self-consciousness, but only lets him [*sic*] see himself [*sic*] through the revelation of the other world. It is a peculiar sensation, this double-consciousness, this sense of always looking at one's self through the eyes of others, of measuring one's soul by the tape of a world that looks on in amused contempt and pity. One ever feels his [*sic*] twoness—an American, a Negro; two souls, two thoughts, two unreconciled strivings; two warring ideals in one dark body, whose dogged strength alone keeps its from being torn asunder.[24]

Insofar as "psychic sensitivity is brutalized by oppression," chained to survival, and confined to inconceivable otherness, conversion releases, heals, and liberates. Conversion releases the psyche from "distorted and alienated" affective or social or aesthetic patterns of experience. "A true healing of the psyche would dissolve the affective wounds that block sustained self-transcendence."[25] For the Black woman or man, psychic conversion is the healing of distortions, hatreds, and alienations from one's own Black flesh, Black self, and Black community. Psychic conversion, then, is realized as the capacity to interpret accurately the most basic symbols of Black human be-ing.[26] The woman or man of converted psyche is free *intentionally* to participate in the constitution of her or his own personhood and to participate in the creation of a human world. Conversion liberates insofar as the woman or man of converted psyche is freed from the labyrinth of doubleness, to recover and to actuate meaning and value.

Foundations, then, involves a theologian's conscious and deliberate decision about whom and what a theologian affirms, and whom and what a theologian disaffirms. Foundations implies a conscious and deliberate decision about a theologian's horizon or worldview, cultural and religious perspective. Foundations calls for a theologian's deliberate decision about knowing, objectivity, and reality; about how (in systematics) true doctrines will be reconciled with one another; about how those doctrines are to be related to the findings and conclusions of modern science, philosophy, and history; about how those doctrines will be effectively communicated within plural cultural contexts.[27]

Foundations is the consolidation of the transformation, the change begun in and achieved in dialectic. There is a change in the results of research, interpretation, history, and dialectic—in the arguments or questions or categories a theologian espouses. Just as importantly, there is "a fundamental and momentous change in the human reality that a theologian is." It is to that fundamental and momentous change we refer when we say, 'We *are* our foundations.' Foundations, then, pertains not to the *products* of culture, but to those principles that create, purify, preserve, develop, and transmit culture; that are violated in its decline and decay—human persons, women and men. Foundations pertains to the human subject: to the methodical, concrete, dynamic unfolding of human attentiveness, intelligence, reasonableness, and responsibility that occurs whenever a theologian of any culture uses her or his mind in appropriate fashion.[28] On this account of foundations, the African American Catholic theologian submits her or his religious, moral, cognitive, and psychic consciousness to the explanatory task of theology. The theologian grounds the theology that is written in the discoveries that she or he has made and verified in the drive for truth and authentic direction in her or his own life and the life of black or African American people.

Section Two: Mediating Black Religious Consciousness

It is, of course, one thing to assert that foundations of a Catholic Theology in an African American perspective are rooted in the religious, moral, intellectual, and psychic conversions of the African American Catholic theologian; it is quite another to draw out concretely the implications of that assertion. The sketch that follows draws out the implications of those conversions in a *base-line religious consciousness* expressed as 'black religion.' This section begins with a rough summary of the complex core of African Traditional Religions that compose the antecedents of *black religion*. Those children, women, and men who survived the Middle Passage did not confront the Americas bereft of religion, culture, value, or worldview. Various sacred cosmological orders came into the Americas and were shattered under the impact of enslavement. Shards or fragments of these sacred orders constitute "root paradigms"[29] that ground *black religion* and the new *black sacred cosmos* it mediates. This new sacred cosmos expressed in black religion is characterized by critical and mystical grasp of the forms and the presence of the sacred on this side of the Atlantic, the blending and fusing of fragments from the canon of traditional West African religio-cultural expression, the borrowing and adaptation of symbols from the dominant culture's religion. Black religion is an historical phenomenon *neither* Protestant *nor* Catholic. Although Africa and African fragments remained normative, Christianity supplied language, images, symbols by which the enslaved peoples interpreted their condition and its meanings. Yet, Christian forms could neither encompass, nor *master* all the religious meanings and intentions of the enslaved black communities. From this basis, I will trace sightings of a most conspicuous fragment, the Kongo cosmogram which emerges at crucial moments in the religions of enslaved Africans in the Americas. As further evidence of blending, fusing, and reconfiguration, I will discuss the spiritual and the ring shout and consider two large theological themes treated in the spirituals: christology and anthropology.

Black Religion

Religion is basic to the whole of human existence, it "tunes human action to an envisaged cosmic order and projects images of cosmic order onto the plane of human experience." In this anthropological approach, religion may be identified as that whole complex of attitudes, convictions, gestures, symbols, rituals, beliefs, and structures which "synthesize[s] a people's ethos—the tone, character, and quality of their life, its moral and aesthetic style and mood—and their worldview."[30] Religion binds the human to the divine in powerful feeling-filled encounter with awesome and fascinating Mystery.[31] Religion thwarts chaos and confounds the absurdity of incomprehensible suffering and evil. It makes whole what is fragmented or broken and binds the wounds of heart and mind, soul and body.

Among Africans, religion, culture, and history were tightly skeined. Often, religious rituals re-enacted the founding of peoples or clans by divine rulers or divinities themselves. From this founding emanated moral injunctions that were mediated by mores and custom, practice and tradition. From this culture came concrete aesthetics in the form of religious art which recapitulated the founding of the peoples; celebrated their divine creation and the creation of their world; and encoded and instructed the proper form of their relations with the Deity, lesser divinities, the ancestors, and the living. Griots told the stories of noble personages, families and clans; thus the oral tradition preserved and transmitted the past. Religion, culture, morality, and history composed an aesthetic whole realized in miniature in each man's, each woman's well lived life.

Traditional African Religions were, and remain, highly particular and specific rather than universal or transcultural. Each cultural-ethnic-linguistic group has its own religion; yet, beneath the rich and exuberant diversity of so many peoples, common modes of apprehension, common patterns of ritual, common values can be discerned. Religion permeated every domain of human life. The whole of the universe radiated and mediated forces of the sacred—the supreme Deity, the divinities, and the spirits.[32] Religion occupied the whole person and the whole of a person's living. The most ordinary and the most extraordinary tasks and activities of daily life, human relationships and social interactions, as well as natural phenomena, were suffused with religious understandings and meanings. In addition to the supreme Deity, the various lesser divinities or gods, Africans had to take into account the ancestors. These honored dead, both those who died long ago and the deceased of more recent memory, remain, even in death, most intimately connected to the living. Because, they are believed capable of intervening in daily affairs, bestowing blessing or meting out punishment, the ancestors must be venerated properly and faithfully according to ritual and custom.[33]

In Traditional African Religions, there are no scriptures to be proclaimed and exegeted, no dogmatic creeds to be studied, assented to, memorized, and observed. Religion "is written not on paper but in people's hearts, minds, oral history, rituals and religious personages like priests, rainmakers, officiating elders and even kings." Ritual and ceremonial practices mark rites of passage or initiation, funerals, births, coronations or installation of chiefs, oath-taking, ordeals, purification, healing, acts of sacrifice and atonement, and divination. Through such rituals breaches in the social fabric are healed, order and harmony are restored to the cosmos. Essential interrelated components of these various rituals include: singing, dancing, drumming; creating and reciting poetry; the use of carved masks, instruments, and figures as well as cloth mannequins. African Traditional Religions mediate salvation and punishment in the here and now. The will of God is exercised in a just way; God is always right. "'God evens things out,' rewarding good to those who follow good conduct, and evil to those who follow evil conduct, and overlooking breaches done accidentally or in error." The moral order of African societies is governed by negative and positive social regulations which regard relations between individuals, and between human beings and the spirits. Hence, African Traditional Religions cultivate and prize moral conduct rooted in aesthetics: a man or woman is said to be good or evil depending upon what he or she does.[34]

In a recent work Jon Butler has argued that chattel slavery "produced an African spiritual holocaust that forever destroyed traditional African religious systems as *systems* and left the slaves remarkably bereft of traditional collective religious practice before 1760."[35] No scholar would argue that the traditional religions of Africa as *systems* (if indeed, that is appropriate nomenclature for them) remained intact under chattel slavery. However, West African peoples did share certain fundamental modes of religious consciousness and religious experience. This field of common consciousness and experience made the remarkable recrudescence of many important and common religious rituals and practices, meanings and values highly probable. Indeed, cogent arguments against the totalizing character of Butler's position have been offered by Herskovitz, Jahn, Thompson, Long, Sobel, and Creel.[36]

Black religion is a very modern term; its poignant advent heralded by exploration, enslavement, coloniality, modernity.[37] It insinuates the alienation of self and community, of the living and the ancestors, of religion and culture, of metaphysics and ontology, of moral and cultural aesthetics. It insinuates the rupture of the sacred cosmos mediated by the traditional religions of West Africa: the fracture, erosion, collapse of discrete religio-cultural, aesthetic-moral meanings and values. Yet, the involuntary and peculiar presence of the cultures of black peoples in the United States demanded an internal response, a religious response. Insofar as the enslaved peoples remembered, blended, fused, and reconfigured practices of their traditional African religions, they constructed new and effective religious rituals as well as new social, aesthetic-moral relations. The fragments of this cultural recollection formed "root paradigms"[38] which fed and nurtured black religious consciousness and grounded "a new black sacred cosmos."[39]

The word black here is *not* an adjective; it neither modifies nor adorns. Rather it signifies and demarcates a dense horizon of meaning and value—a black worldview. The term, "black religion," then, is retrieved from negatory use; and, although the term signifies "opaqueness," "oppugnancy," the reality as experienced *is* tremendous mystery, holy, aweful; the reality as expressed *is* ecstatic, joyous, creative.[40] Black religion is a particular, historical, cultural, spiritual, and, perhaps, divinely revealed phenomenon, "closely bound up with the Christian tradition, [yet] not exhausted in it."[41] Black religion is a graced manifestation of improvising psychic, aesthetic, moral, intellectual, and religious consciousness. In the crucible of history, black religion signified healing, creativity, power, possibility.

The Kongo Cosmogram

The Bakongo peoples were, perhaps, the most numerous among the captured and enslaved.[42] These peoples possessed a religio-cultural tradition dating perhaps as early as the first millennium. The philosophic and visual tradition of the cosmogram has had a decisive and perduring influence on blacks enslaved in the Americas.

The Bakongo "world was profoundly informed by a cosmogram—an ideal balancing of the vitality of the world of the living with the visionariness of the world of the dead."[43] The life, thought, and rituals of Bakongo women and men imitate the great cosmic journey of the sun encoded in cosmogram cruciform [See Figure 1].

The right-hand sphere or corner stands for dawn which, in turn, is the sign of a life beginning. Noon in the uppermost disk or corner, indicates the flourishing of life, the point of most ascendant power. Next, by the inevitable organic process as we know it, come change and flux, the setting of the sun, and death, marked by the left-hand median point of the disk.[44]

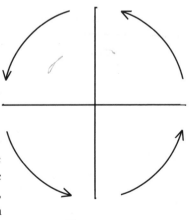

Figure 1

"Bakongo believe and hold it true that man's [*sic*] life has no end, that it constitutes a cycle. The sun, in its rising and setting, is a sign of this cycle, and death is merely a transition in the process of change." Thus, if man or woman lived a good life, he or she could expect to "return within another dawn, emerg[e] from the midnight world, [and be] carried back into the mainstream of the living, in name or body of grandchildren or succeeding generations."[45]

The internalization of this Sacred Cosmos was a crucial aspect of Bakongo socialization. In order to realize its perfect vision, the monotheistic Bakongo sought the aid of a "complex system of *minkisi* (sacred medicines)" which they believe were given by God to humankind. Each Bakongo was to live this movement of the sun in miniature. The brilliance of the sun was to be reflected in the brilliance of a life of wisdom and justice in the midst of the imperfect world of the living.[46]

The Spirituals

The formal Christianization of the enslaved Africans in the United States is a disputed question. Scholars cannot isolate the precise points of encounter between those authentic efforts to evangelize and catechize the enslaved peoples which lead to the appearance of Black Christian churches.[47] What we know unequivocally is: the preaching of salvation in Jesus of Nazareth, Son of God, and Christ inevitably had a decisive impact on the enslaved peoples. What I venture about the encounter is this: *the religious sensibilities of the enslaved peoples projected a religious reality in which Christianity is sublated by the reconfigured elements of traditional West African religions.* At the same time, because so very much of the interior life of the enslaved peoples—their feelings and hopes, desires and aspirations, religious and cultural practices, and interpretations and reflections—were masked or hidden from the master class, indeed, from nearly all Whites, it is not possible to pronounce with any certainty the burial of the African gods and the complete disappearance of the traditional religions. When the enslaved peoples moaned

> *I've been 'buked an' I've been scorned*
> *Dere is trouble all over dis worl'*
> *Ain' gwine lay my 'ligion down*
> *Ain' gwine lay my 'ligion down*

we can never be sure *which* religion they refused to surrender.[48]

Historians and cultural anthropologists generally agree that on the plantations, religion was the sphere in which the enslaved Africans were able to exercise some measure of autonomy and freedom in intelligence, action, and creativity. Still, they did so often at the risk of grave punishment.[49] On some plantations, the enslaved peoples were permitted to hold independent and, sometimes, unsupervised worship services; on others, they attended White churches, sitting or standing in designated areas. On still other plantations, the enslaved people were punished for praying and singing. Yet, they persisted and fashioned for themselves "an inner world, a scale of values and fixed points of vantage from which to judge the world around them and themselves."[50]

Simon Brown, born into slavery in 1843 and initiated at an early age into the circle of religio-cultural practices created by the enslaved peoples, points out some differences between Christianity practiced by the Africans (black or African American Christianity) and the Christianity practiced by the master class.

> I use' to drive my Massa's family in town to church, in the "two-horse surrey," on a Sunday. I had to sit upstairs with the other slaves. We act like we enjoy' the services, but we didn't…the slave' had they Christian religion too, an' it wasn't cole and "Proper," like the white folk' church. [But] The fact is, the black folk in my day didn't even have a church. They meet in a cabin in the cole weather an' outdoors, under a tree or a "brush arbor" in the summertime. Sometimes the Massa's preacher would "talk" at the meetin's 'bout bein' obedient to our massas an' good servants, an' 'bout goin' to heaven when we die'…. But, oh, my, when my people got together to "Wishop" God, the Spirit would "move in the meetin'!"…
>
> The folk' would sing an' pray an' "testify," an' clap they han's, jus' as if God was right there in the midst of them. He wasn't way off, up in the sky: He was a-seein' everybody an' a-listen' to ever' word an' a-promisin' to "let His love come down." My people would be so burden' down with they trials an' tribulations, an' broken hearts, that I seen them break down an' cry like babies…. Yes sir, there was no pretendin' in those prayer-meetin's. There was a livin' faith in a jus' God who would one day answer the cries of his poor black chillen an' deliver them from they enemies. But they never say a word to they white folks 'bout this *kine of faith.*[51]

A singular indication of this "kine of faith," of black religion as African American Christianity was the spiritual. Although there is eyewitness testimony regarding religious and secular songs made by the enslaved Africans in the late eighteenth century, widespread "discovery" of the spiritual coincides with the Civil War.[52] James Weldon Johnson, poet, literary critic, and foremost collector of these noble Black psalms, believed that many were the work of highly gifted individuals, whom he called in a most celebrated poem, "black and unknown bards."[53] The folklorist Zora Neale Hurston maintained that the spirituals are "Negro religious songs, sung by a group, and a group bent on expression of feelings and not on sound effects."[54]

When questioned about their method of composing their religious songs, enslaved men and women often replied: "De Lord jes' put hit en our mouf. We is ignorant, and de Lord puts ebry word we says en our mouf."[55] One informant put it this way:

> I'll tell you; it's dis way. My master call me up and order me a short peck of corn and a hundred lash. My friends see it and is sorry for me. When dey come to de praise meeting dat night dey sing about it. Some's very good singers and know how;—dey work it in, work it in, you know; till dey get it right; and dat's de way.[56]

An emancipated woman from Kentucky insisted that the spirituals were formed from the material of traditional African tunes and familiar songs. Listen to her description of the process by which spirituals were made:

> Us ole head use ter make 'em on de spurn of de moment, after we wressle wid de Spirit and come thoo. But the tunes was brung from Africa by our grandaddies. Dey was jis 'miliar song...dey calls 'em spirituals, case de Holy Spirit done revealed 'em to 'em. Some say Moss Jesus taught 'em, and I's seed 'em start in meetin'. We'd all be at the 'prayer house' de Lord's Day and de white preacher he'd splain de word and read whar Ezekiel done say—
> Dry bones gwine ter lib again.
> And, honey, de Lord would come a-shining thoo dem pages and revive dis ole [woman's] heart, and I'd jump up dar and den and holler and shout and sing and pat, and dey would all cotch de words...dey's all take it up and keep at it, and keep a-addin' to it and den it would be a spiritual.[57]

What is a spiritual? A spiritual may be defined as the moaned or sung utterance of an enslaved African American in response to or about a given social or religious experience that had communal and/

or universal application. In and through song, one man's or woman's experience of sorrow or shout of jubilation became that of a people. But without a doubt, the spirituals are gifts of the Spirit.

In creation and performance, the spirituals are marked by flexibility, spontaneity, and improvisation. The pattern of call-response allowed for the rhythmic weaving or manipulation of time, text, and pitch; while, the response or repetitive chorus provided a recognizable and stable foundation for the extemporized lines of the soloist or leader.[58] Moreover, the creation and performance of the spirituals were nourished by the African disposition for aesthetic performance— for doing the beautiful—in dance, in song, in poetry making, in instrumentalizing. The spirituals are simple, yet not simplistic; they possess what African American Catholic liturgist Clarence Rivers has called magnitude.[59] With their dense mediation of unimaginable anguish as well as deep joy, thick melodic power, the songs control the singer who must bow to the flash of the Spirit.

The spirituals give access to the "experience[s], expression[s], motivations, intentions, behaviors, styles, and rhythms" of African American religio-cultural life.[60] They are a window on the religious, social, aesthetic, emotional, and psychic worldview of a people. They are best appreciated when we imagine them, not concertized with dissonances "ironed out," but moaned in jagged irregular harmony, falsetto breaking in and keys changing with emotion.[61] The spirituals are best understood when we take them off the stage and return them to their natural, ceremonial, or ritual settings— rude cabins of rough wooden planks, "woods, gullies, ravines, and thickets" (aptly called brush arbors or hush arbors), overturned iron pots nearby.[62] The songs are linked to adaptations of African religious rituals, including funeral and burial ceremonies. Invariably these rites included hand clapping or the stomping of feet, which would have compensated on many plantations for the outlawed drum. However, the spiritual is linked most intimately to the shuffling of the *ring shout.*

A distinct form of worship, the ring shout is basically a dancing-singing phenomenon in which the song is *danced* with the whole body—hands, feet, shoulders, hips. When the spiritual is sounded, the ring-shout begins. The dancers form a circle and move *counterclockwise* in a ring, first by walking slowly, and then by shuffling— the foot just slightly lifted from the floor. Sometimes the people danced silently; most often they sang the chorus of the spiritual as they shuffled; at other times, the entire song itself is sung by the dancers. Frequently, a group of the best singers and of tired shouters stand at the side of the room to 'base' the others, singing the body or stanzas of the song and clapping their hands. The dancing and singing would increase in intensity and energy and sometimes went on for hours; and, sometimes, in their religious fervor, the people became possessed by spirits.[63]

The Bakongo believe that the "combined force of singing Ki-Kongo words and tracing in appropriate media the ritually designated 'point' or 'mark' of contact between the worlds will result in the descent of God's power."[64] As the enslaved peoples sang and moved counterclockwise in a ring, they danced such a 'point' or 'mark'; they danced the Kongo cosmogram, reinscribing it on their minds and hearts and the minds and hearts of their children. The Ki-Kongo words were lost, but the enslaved peoples sang: "I got my religion from out the sun, I clapped my hands and began to run"; or "He made the sun to shine by day, He made the sun to show the way"; or "Watch the Sun, how steady she runs, Don't let her catch you with your work undone." John Lovell catalogs these songs among those that refer to nature and God's power over nature. But, the cosmogram's intimate connection to the sun permits a rich reading of the origin and intent of these songs, for participation in the ring-shout re-enacted the cosmic journey of the sun. Thus, in dance, the Africans remembered, preserved, and transmitted a cherished religious, aesthetico-moral, and social vision of the world that dictated a life of morality and beauty.

Men and women who enjoyed visions and religious experiences of seemingly Christian derivation drew on cosmogramic images for interpretation: "I saw, as it were, a ladder. It was more like a pole with rungs on it let down from heaven, and it reached from heaven to earth. I was on the bottom rung, and somebody was on every rung, climbing upward...."[65] The image of a ladder or pole let down from heaven to earth restates the classical Kongo teaching of the connection and communication between the world of the living and the world of the dead.

There is suggestive evidence linking the cosmogram to the spiritual, "Wade in the Water." In "How the Slaves Worshipped," Simon Brown relates some interesting features of [Christian] baptismal ceremonies. "New converts were made ready for baptizing...the First

Sunday, down by the Mill Pond." Wearing long white gowns, male and female candidates would gather together and march down to the edge of the pond to wait for the service to begin. "One of the deacons holding a long staff built like a cross…would wade out into the water, using his staff as a sounding stick." When the deacon located the "proper depth he'd drive [the staff] down hard into the bottom."[66] As the baptizing commenced, the people sang

> *Wade in the water, Children;*
> *Oh, wade in the water, chillen;*
> *Wade in the water, children;*
> *God's going to trouble the water.*

The deacon's cross-shaped staff would have reminded enslaved Bakongo men and women and their children of the Kongo cosmogram. The cross-shaped staff [†] symbolized the four moments of the sun, the four corners of the earth, the four winds of heaven. It signified the boundary line, *kalunga*, or the sea that divides the world of the living from the world of the dead. One line of the cross-shaped staff [†] "represents the boundary; the other is ambivalently both the path leading across the boundary," in this instance the pond, the waters of baptism; "*and* the vertical path of power linking 'the above' with 'the below.' This relationship, in turn, is polyvalent, since it refers to God and man [*sic*], God and the dead, and the living and the dead."[67] To the Bakongo, the candidates' immersion in the water was a transversing of this boundary and mystical communication with the ancestors, with the other world. Often, the candidate came up out of the water shouting, a clear sign of that communion. The meaning of the Bakongo notion of *kalunga*, the boundary line that demarcates the kingdom of the dead from the land of the living, is not so much dissolved or conflated in the baptismal water (the Jordan). Rather, the meaning of *kalunga* sublates the meaning of baptismal water ascribing to it even more spiritual and moral significance.

Thompson reports that members of the Lemba society of healers instructed initiates to stand on a cross chalked on the ground, a variant of the cosmogram. Those who stood on the intersection of the point were said to be "fully capable of governing people, knew the nature of the world, [and] had mastered the meaning of life and

death." The initiates were empowered with knowledge from both
worlds; they could conduct and direct themselves and advise others
accordingly.[68] It is not too much to suggest that this meaning is encoded in the words of this spiritual: "Better min', my brother, how
you walk on the cross, I feel like my time ain't long/Your foot might
slip and your soul get lost, I feel like my time ain't long."

The Kongo cosmogram is a protean symbol. The deacon's cross-
shaped staff with its cosmogramic semblance held special meaning
for the enslaved peoples familiar with or initiated into Bakongo rituals. There is little doubt that, among the candidates for baptism and
those enslaved folk who obtained passes and came to pray for and
support the new converts, there were Christian believers. To be sure,
these believers would have participated in making their own Christianity; for the way the enslaved folk would and could follow Jesus
necessarily was unique. Yet, such Christian symbol and practice provided a cover for those, whether newly arrived or second generation,
enslaved Africans who passed on complex codes and signs to sustain
themselves in a situation of oppression. At the same time, these African (e.g., Bakongo or Angolan) codes and signs sublate symbol and
practice and invest them with new (i.e., African) meanings awakening unique sentiments and responses. In this sublation, the fragments
of traditional African religio-cultural heritages function as *root paradigms* in the emergence of a crucial stratum of African American
Christianity.

It is important to recall that the enslaved peoples were forbidden
to learn to read and to write. It is equally important to recall that
there is ample evidence that many African cultural-ethnic linguistic
groups read and wrote.[69] But, those enslaved African men and women
in the United States caught defying these injunctions risked severe
punishment. Many slaveholders viciously beat enslaved men and
women whom they found reading; and some slaveholders even cut
the forefinger from the right hand of slaves whom they caught, or
suspected of, writing. The initial encounter of the enslaved Africans
with the Bible came, not so much by *reading*, as by hearing. Thus, in
creating the spirituals, singers drew selectively on material "picked
up...rather than read from" the Hebrew and Christian Scriptures.[70]
The vocabulary, characters, places, and events sung in the spirituals
"reflect the transformation of the Book Religion of the dominant

peoples"[71] into the prophetic, apocalyptic, emancipatory religion of the enslaved. And, what is most astonishing, perhaps cannot be argued: *the conversion of the God of the slave masters to the cause of the emancipation of the enslaved.*[72]

In the spirituals, *a history of salvation* takes place before our very eyes; indeed, each of us is included in it. Each of us is commissioned to "Go and tell on the Mountain, that Jesus Christ is born"! Each of us climbs "Jacob's Ladder" as "Every round goes higher and higher." Each of us stands awed to see what Ezekiel sees: the big wheel running by faith, the little wheel running by the grace of God, a wheel within a wheel. And, each of us must answer the question, "Were you there when they crucified my Lord?"

Biblical places most conspicuous in the spirituals include: the Jordan: the river dividing time and eternity, slave land and free land; Egypt: the land from which the freed people emerge, the land leading to the wilderness; the Red Sea: "God's sink of judgment upon pursuers of the chosen people; Canann: free and promised land; and Galilee: the home country of Jesus Christ."[73] The people of the Old Testament who appear most in spirituals include: Adam and Eve, Methuselah, Noah, Abraham, Isaac, Joseph, Jacob, Moses and the Israelites, Pharaoh, Joshua, Samson, David, Ezekiel, Jonah, Daniel, and the three Hebrew Children—Shadrach, Meshach, and Abednego.

The Jesus of the spirituals is an intimate friend of the enslaved peoples. His birth, crucifixion, death, and resurrection are familiar details to the makers of the spirituals. Other people of the New Testament most frequently cited in the spirituals include: Mary, the mother of Jesus; John the Baptist; the apostles John, Peter, Thomas, and Paul; Nicodemus; Mary and Martha of Bethany; Mary Magdalen; Lazarus, Dives, and Pilate.[74]

The language employed in the spirituals is intensely poetic and expressive, decorative and poignant. The vocabulary is filled with vivid simile, creative and effective juxtaposition of images and metaphor. Rooted in the historical experience of oppression, this highly charged symbolic language is most fundamentally a language of joy and mysticism in the midst of survival and resistance.

The language of the spirituals connote *anamnesis, charisma, midrash,* and an *eschatology.* In language of *anamnesis* or memory, the spirituals venerate and honor the ancestors, the more than twenty million African women and men who disappeared in the Middle Passage, whose bones, which litter the floor of the Atlantic, shall surely rise on the last day to meet the Christ; the mother, father, brother, and sister sold away at whim. In *charismatic* language, the spirituals sing openly and confidently of the power and gifts of the Spirit to bring life out of death and despair, to bring health and wholeness out of pain, to pour joy into broken hearts. In the language of *midrash*, the spirituals reshape, re-tell, and conflate the characters and stories, parables and pericopes, events and miracles of the Hebrew and Christian Scriptures. These songs tell the mercy of God anew and testify to the ways in which the enslaved people met God in the slave quarter, at the whipping post, on the auction block, in the hush arbor, in the midnight flight to freedom. In *eschatological* language, the spirituals weave the stories of women and men hoping and trusting in the promises of the Kingdom of God. The spirituals are expectant and evocative—building a new place of life and peace for those oppressed by the pain and tribulations of slavery.

The spirituals dialogue with the Scriptures, laying the religious and social experiences of the enslaved Africans beside those of the Biblical Hebrews, with the same expectation that the Lord God of Hosts would deliver them and comfort them. When the prophet Jeremiah moans: "My grief is beyond healing, my heart is sick within me.... For the wound of the daughter of my people is my heart wounded, I mourn, and dismay has taken hold on me. Is there no balm in Gilead?" (8: 18, 21-22) The enslaved singer retorts:

> There is a balm in Gilead to make the wounded whole
> There is a balm in Gilead to heal the sin-sick soul
> Sometimes I feel discouraged an' think my work in vain
> But then the Holy Spirit revives my soul again.

Jesus tells the parable of rich Dives and poor Lazarus. When Lazarus died, he was carried by angels to Abraham's bosom; but Dives is sent to eternal punishment in hell. Tormented in the flames, Dives begs Abraham for mercy: "[S]end Lazarus to dip the end of his finger in water and cool my tongue." Abraham reminds Dives that there is a great chasm between those who have relished the good things in this life while abusing the poor who now enjoy the favors of God (Luke 16: 19-31). Standing in the rude slave cabin, the maker of the spiritual, looked at the plantation owners "big house" and nodded ever so wisely at the working of divine justice and power. The anonymous singer called out in trust, in confidence, and in warning:

> *Poor old Lazarus, poor as I, Don't you see? Don't you see?*
> *Poor old Lazarus, poor as I, Don't you see? Don't you see?*
> *Poor old Lazarus, poor as I, When he died had a home on high.*
> *He had a home in-a-that Rock, Don't you see?*
>
> *Rich man, Dives, lived so well, Don't you see? Don't you see?*
> *Rich man, Dives, lived so well, Don't you see? Don't you see?*
> *Rich man, Dives, lived so well, When he died found a home in hell,*
> *He had no home in that Rock, Don't you see?*

The spirituals employ highly self-critical language. The maker of the spiritual never romanticizes the African American. The maker of the spiritual admits what the slave holders refuse to admit—the enslaved man and woman is a *human being* who can and does sin against God and neighbor. The spiritual admonishes 'the would be Christian' to be conscious and critical of content and intentionality in speech, in song, and in joy.

> *You got give account in de Judgment, you'd better min'.*
> *You'd better min' how you talk,*
> *You'd better min' what you talkin' about.*
>   *You got give account in de Judgment, you'd better min'.*
> *You'd better min' how you sing,*
> *You'd better min' what you sing about.*
> *You'd better min' how you shout,*
> *You'd better min' what you shout about.*

The need for forgiveness, for mercy, for support that only prayer can bring is acknowledged in the spiritual:

> *not my brother, nor my sister,*
> *not the preacher, nor the deacon,*
> *not my father, nor my mother,*
> *not the stranger, nor my neighbor,*
> *but it's me, O Lord, standin' in the need of prayer.*

In the desire to be made more holy, more faithful, more humble, more righteous, the singer calls out to the Lord: "Come by here, somebody needs you, Lord, somebody needs a blessing."

The spirituals are unambiguously clear that 'none but the righteous shall see God' and that the wicked shall be punished, yet, these prayer-psalms are never tainted with the brush of hatred. Indeed, the spirituals are singularly free of all references to vengeance. Yet, from a privileged hermeneutical stance emerging from massive suffering, the enslaved peoples turned a critical eye on the hypocrisy of the Christianity of the slaveholders.[75] One former slave offers this report:

> I often heard select portions of the Scriptures read.... On Sunday we always had one sermon prepared expressly for the colored people.... So great was the similarity of texts that they are always fresh in memory: "Servants, be obedient to your masters—not with eye-service, as men-pleasers." "He that knoweth his master's will and doeth it not, shall be beaten with many stripes"; and some of this class.... One very kind-hearted clergyman...was very popular with the coloured people. But after he had preached a sermon from the Bible that it was the will of Heaven from all eternity that we should be slaves, and our masters be our owners many of us left them, considering, like the doubting disciple of old, "This is a hard saying, who can hear it."[76]

The enslaved peoples signified more than their rejection of *ersatz Christianity* in this most ironic of refrains: "Everybody talkin' 'bout heaven ain' a-goin' there." And there is no other way to read any other meaning into these words: "You may be a white man, White as the drifting snow, If your soul ain't been converted, To Hell you're sure to go."

Adamant that we not misunderstand the intention of spirituals that seem simple, John Lovell offers an insightful analysis of "Lord, I want to be a Christian."

> *Lord, I want to be a Christian in my heart, in-a my heart,*
> *Lord, I want to be a Christian in my heart,*
>   *Lord, I want to be more loving in my heart, in-a my heart,*
>   *Lord, I want to be more loving in my heart,*
> *Lord, I want to be more holy in my heart, in-a my heart,*
> *Lord, I want to be more holy in my heart,*
>   *Lord, I want to be like Jesus in my heart, in-a my heart,*
>   *Lord, I want to be like Jesus in my heart.*

The critical intention of the song is found in the phrase—*in-a my heart.* This phrase, Lovell maintains, indicates that a woman or man desires to be a "true believer...not a surface operator, and intends to carry out in every respect the obligations and responsibilities of the Christian."[77] The practice of Christianity, the lived Christian life is not something ethereal or ahistorical, rather it is deeply embedded in concrete history, in time and space. This spiritual "makes known its disgust with phony, insincere Christians...who practice selfishness and brutality...who go to church on Sunday morning and come home and beat their slaves on Sunday afternoon."[78] Thus, through *coded* or *masked* language, the spiritual distinguishes authentic Christian experience and true religious practice from fraudulent and inauthentic Christian practice; it resists any *kerygma* that debases black humanity. At the same time, even as the spiritual protectively masks its criticism, it uncovers the precarious hermeneutical situation of the slaveholders who pressed Christianity into ideological service. Southern slaveholders treated the relation of masters and slaves as divinely ordained and disregarded the transforming effect of Baptism on these relations, preferring the economic to the sacramental. The spirituals protest this heretical and perverse Christianity. Of the power of the spirituals, Frederick Douglass writes

> I have sometimes thought, that the mere hearing of these songs would do more to impress truly spiritual-minded men and women with the soul crushing and death-dealing character of slavery, than the reading of whole volumes of its mere physical cruelties. They speak to the heart and to the soul of the thoughtful.... Every tone was a testimony against slavery, and a prayer to God for deliverance from chains.[79]

The Jesus of the Spirituals

In the spirituals, James Cone asserts, theology becomes Christology.[80] Jesus is the center, text, and subtext of the enslaved peoples' religion. These songs do not offer speculation on the nature of the humanity and divinity of Jesus of Nazareth or the hypostatic union, the metaphysics of the black sacred cosmos directed their attention elsewhere. The power of Jesus was discerned in his identification with them in their situation: "Did you ever see the like before, King Jesus preaching to the poor/ My Lord's done just what he said, Healed the sick and rais'd the dead." Jesus demonstrated the ability to help the navigate suffering and pain, evil and affliction with dignity. Jesus could be found in vision through prayer: "Ef you want to see Jesus, Go in de Wilderness" or "King Jesus is a-listenin' all day long, To hear some sinner pray." The enslaved folk like the poor of the Christian gospels learned to expect his response. Like Kongo *nkisi* or sacred medicine, the very name of Jesus delighted, instructed, and healed: "I love Jesus for his name's so sweet./ I'm just now from the fountain, His name's so sweet"; "Jesus Christ is first and last, No man works like him"; "Fix me, Jesus, fix me"; "I know the Lord has laid his hands on me."

The enslaved peoples assume a close and familiar relationship with Jesus. He is their "rock in a weary lan,' " their "shelter in a storm," and "a little talk with Jesus, Makes it right." He is addressed as a cherished friend who will walk with them through the hardships of a hard life:

> I want Jesus to walk with me;
> I want Jesus to walk with me;
> All along my pilgrim journey,
> Lord, I want Jesus to walk with me.
>
> In my trials, Lord walk with me;
> In my trials, Lord walk with me;
> When my heart is almost breaking,
> Lord, I want Jesus to walk with me.
>
> When I'm in trouble, Lord walk with me;
> When I'm in trouble, Lord walk with me;
> When my head is bowed in sorrow,
> Lord, I want Jesus to walk with me.

It is Jesus who is a comforter in time of trouble and in the most intimate moments of joy or anguish, we hear the cry: "Give me Jesus, Give me Jesus, You may have all this world, Give me Jesus."

Freedom was the dominant theme of the religion that emerged from within the circle of culture created by the enslaved peoples. The struggle for freedom did not splinter or subdivide into its distinct dimensions—for example, the political *or* social *or* spiritual *or* religious. Rather, the freedom for which the enslaved peoples longed, struggled, fought, and died was, at once, political *and* social, psychic *and* spiritual, metaphysical *and* ontological, this-worldly *and* otherworldly.[81]

The enslaved Africans understood Jesus Christ as the Bringer of freedom, as their Savior. This understanding was derived from two primary sources: a subtle grasp of the Scriptures and the circle of culture that gave us B'rer Rabbit, B'rer Fox, and B'rer Mockin' Bird; Ole Sister, High John de Conquer and Stackolee; Anansi and King Buzzard.[82] From this circle of culture came the trickster, the legendary and mythic heroes and 'bad men' who would not be bested. From this circle of culture came enslaved and free men and women who fought with every means at their disposal for freedom, for emancipation.

Against the conscious efforts of slaveholders and the institution that sustained them, Jesus came to mean freedom. As Howard Thurman observes, "It was dangerous to let the slave understand that the life and teachings of Jesus meant freedom for the captive and release for those held in economic, social, and political bondage."[83] To understand the fearless and dangerous Jesus was to break the spell cast by the prevailing dominative consciousness—to break with a slave mentality. To understand the fearless and dangerous Jesus was to release the Word of God from the grip of the slave holders and set it free working in the midst of those yearning to be free.

> *Woke Up This Morning with my mind, And it was stayed,*
> *Stayed on Jesus.*
> *Can't hate your neighbor in you mind, If you keep it stayed,*
> *Stayed on Jesus.*
>
> *Makes you love everybody with your mind, When you keep it stayed,*
> *Stayed on Jesus.*
> *The Devil can't catch you in your mind, If you keep it stayed,*
> *Stayed on Jesus.*
>
> *Jesus is the captain in you mind, When you keep it stayed,*
> *Stayed on Jesus*

During the most recent Civil Rights Movement of the 1950s, when this spiritual was sung, the word *freedom* was substituted and interchanged with the name of *Jesus.* This substitution was in keeping with the intentionality and the spirit of the enslaved peoples' grasp of the meaning and message of Jesus. Long before the publications of Ernst Käsemann or Gustavo Gutiérrez or James Cone, for the oppressed enslaved African peoples in the United States, Jesus *meant* freedom, Jesus *was* freedom.[84]

It is not surprising that the spirituals focus on the suffering, the crucifixion, and death of Jesus. The enslaved folk knew what it meant to suffer and in Jesus' suffering and death they saw their own experience. Narratives about enslavement report an especially vicious form of brutality in which an enslaved man or woman would be *staked*. The enslaved man or woman would be forced to lie face down on the ground, with arms and legs extended and tied to stakes. Then, the person would be flogged. Another form of this punishment required that the enslaved man's or woman's "hands would be tied together with a rope, which was then thrown over the limb of a tree or over a beam." Then the person would be "pulled up till the toes only just reached the ground, feet tied together, and a rail or fence thrust between the legs with a weight on it to keep the body at full stretch."[85] This form of punishment was not uncommon. We do not know whether it gave rise to the following spiritual, but in this lament the enslaved folk poured out in anguish for Jesus, that transcended the limitations of time and space. Jesus stood with them in their sufferings, they stood with Jesus in his.

> *They nail my Jesus down,*
> *They put him on the crown of thorns*
> *O see my Jesus hangin' high!*
> *He look so pale an' bleed so free:*
> *O don't you think it was a shame,*
> *He hung three hours in dreadful pain?*

Jesus was the answer to prayers for freedom; he was "God's Black Slave who had come to put an end to human bondage."[86] The resurrection of Jesus meant that death would not be the last word, that slavery would not be the last word. The God who vindicated Jesus would vindicate the enslaved peoples and that vindication was, at once, *eschatological* and *historical, other-worldly* and *this-worldly*.

Heaven was the place the enslaved people would finally "lay down the heavy load." Heaven was the site of "bright mansions above." Here there would be no more whippings, no more back-breaking labor from sunup to sundown. Here there would be no more hunger and thirst, no more sorrow and pain: "No more hard trial in de kingdom; no more tribulation, no more parting, no more quarreling, backbiting in de kingdom." Heaven is vividly portrayed: pearly gates, golden streets, long white robes, shoes, and wings! Moreover, heaven is peopled with the mother and father, sister and brother, friends and other kin folk who had been sold away or died. Heaven is home.

> *Children, we shall be free*
> *When the Lord shall appear.*
> *Give ease to the sick, give sight to the blind,*
> *Enable the cripple to walk;*
> *He'll raise the dead from under the earth,*
> *And give them permission to talk.*

To paraphrase Walter Benjamin, the spirituals are shot through with chips of messianic time. In this spiritual, anyone familiar with the Hebrew and Christian Scriptures apprehends those signs (Isaiah 61:1-2, 58:6; Luke: 4:18-19). Like Isaiah's announcement, the spiritual testifies to a deep longing for concrete salvation, for the realization of the hopes and dreams of a long oppressed people, for a new age in which the powerful slaveholders are vanquished, sinners punished, and the righteous rewarded. Like the men and women of the Lucan narrative, the spiritual longs for the miracles and appearance of Jesus. Freedom will mean the end of the auction block, the driver's lash, no more weeping. Freedom will mean reunion, not only with the beloved dead who may now be honored fully, but also with those who have run away or escaped chattel slavery. Jesus was God's inbreaking and transformation of their historical condition. To these women and men he was "a god of compassion and suffering, a promulgator of freedom and peace and opportunity, a son of an omnipotent Father"[87] who would bring about their historic liberation.

Anthropology: Freedom and Human Being

For the oppressed enslaved Africans freedom, emancipation, liberation, and salvation were inseparably linked. Freedom meant emancipation: the elimination of the status and conditions of enslavement and oppression. Freedom, as emancipation from bondage, was a concrete, vital, and present reality intimately linked to any notion of liberation and salvation. Liberation projected the possibility of creative and personal exercise of freedom. Salvation was not grounded in some distant future; salvation occurred in the here and now; it occurred on earth as well as in the hereafter.

The spirituals grasp the Biblical story of *exodus* as the paradigmatic experience of God's unmeasured act of love and liberation in history. The most renowned and cherished of all the spirituals tells the ancient story of the oppression, emancipation, liberation, and salvation of the Hebrew people. The enslaved singers reappropriated their own experience of capture, handling, oppression, and enslavement in light of this paradigm. Long before Latin American liberation theology called us to attend to the overlooked theme of liberation as Jesus' most basic message (Luke 4: 16-30), oppressed and enslaved African peoples in the United States sang out in defiance and confidence, in hope and in hunger, the revelation they had received from the Lord of Hosts:

> *When Israel was in Egypt's land, Let my people go;*
> *Oppressed so hard they could not stand, Let my people go.*
> *Go down Moses, way down in Egypt's land;*
> *Tell old Pharaoh to let my people go.*
>
> *The Lord told Moses what to do, Let my people go;*
> *To lead the children of Israel through, Let my people go.*
>
> *They journeyed on at God's command, Let my people go;*
> *And came at length to Canaan's land, Let my people go.*
>
> *Oh let us all from bondage flee, Let my people go.*
> *And let us all in Christ be free, Let my people go.*
>
> *We need not always weep and moan, Let my people go.*
> *And wear these slavery chains forlorn.*

The enslaved Africans place their experience alongside that of the enslaved Hebrews. Faithful to the Hebrew narrative, the spiritual sings God as the author and initiator of the people's freedom and emancipation. God hears the cries and anguish of the people. God instructs Moses to lead them from Egypt, through the wilderness, and finally into the promised land. Egypt is a land of pain and suffering, of enslavement and oppression; the peoples' bondage is physical, political, economic, and spiritual. As the enslaved Africans sing the desire of the enslaved Hebrews for freedom, they sing their own desires. The song and the singer yearn for "the promised land" of Canaan with its new physical, political, economic, and spiritual possibilities. The song and the enslaved singer create a heaven that is a site of freedom. It is a place of *real community*. Here the enslaved man and woman is reunited with the mother and father, the sister and brother who had been sold away. Here, the enslaved man and woman enjoys the intimate and comfortable companionship of Jesus and his Father: "Gwine to argue wid de father and chatter wid de son"; "I'm going to walk with (talk with, live with, see) King Jesus...*myself.*"[88]

Finally, the spirituals manifest the moral and religious self-transcendence of a people in bondage, but whose song broke the shackles from their minds, their hearts, their souls. Men and women, consigned to slavery in perpetuity, sang:

> *Oh Freedom, Oh Freedom, Oh Freedom over me,*
> *And before I'd be a slave, I'll be buried in my grave,*
> *And go home to my Lord and be free.*

Just as the author of the slave narrative quite literally wrote himself and herself into human being, into active existence, so too, the maker of the spiritual quite literally sang himself and herself into human being, into active existence. There is an implicit theological anthropology in the spirituals and this particular song renders it most effectively. The humanity of the enslaved Africans was much disputed. More theologically liberal churches held that the enslaved Africans had three-fifths of a soul; more theologically conservative church were not sure if the Africans had souls at all. Indeed, baptism was delayed by Anglicans for several decades in colonial Virginia because slave holders believed they could not enslave other Christians.

The spirituals that sing of freedom insist that although effectively (i.e., personally or practically or politically or economically) the slave could not control his and her own destiny, person or work or travel, the enslaved man or woman was *free.* "Oh, Freedom" defies the degradation of chattel slavery and honored the enslaved man and woman's steadfast refusal to interiorize such degradation. This song revealed and nurtured the enslaved singer's sense of self-worth and personal dignity. Rather than lose self, the enslaved man or woman prefers to embrace death. This spiritual expressed and sustained a worldview out of which the slave might live, think, move, and act *free.*

This recursive and archaeological excavation discloses some representative manifestations or fragments that survived the diasporic collapse of sacred cosmological orders mediated by traditional religions of Africa. The selection and reconfiguration of blended and fused fragments was the work of that *baseline religious consciousness,* generative, of black religion, and then, of the distinctive African reception of the Christian message in the United States. On this account, religious consciousness is the crucial mediation of African American personal and communal self-transcendence and transformation. The apprehension, understanding, and judgment of that consciousness and its significations—signs, symbols, images, and preconceptual forms—grounds African American Catholic theologizing.

Section Three:
Marks of an African American Catholic Theological Mediation

A Catholic theology grounded in African American religious experience and consciousness, taking as its point of departure the *complex* and *hard* experience of being *black Catholic* in the United States, and accountable in interpretation to the word of God in and for this situation awaits full articulation.[89] Yet, given the notion of foundations advanced in the first section and the recursive findings of the second, it is possible to suggest *seven* marks or features of such a theology.

1. Since black or African American culture has been nourished primarily by religious consciousness, a Catholic theological mediation in African American perspective will be grounded in the religious experience and religious consciousness of black or African American peoples. Because of the history of crude and imperious treatment of the religions and cultures of black peoples in the United States, at the level of critical thought, this theology will recognize and acknowledge 'black religious experience' as the crucial locus and resource for theologizing.

2. A Catholic theological mediation in black or African American perspective will depend upon engagement and critical appropriation of the historical, religious, cultural, social, moral, psychic experience of *being black* and of *black being*. The term *blackness* signifies color, culture, and consciousness; the phrase *black experience* insinuates the compound-complex historical, religious, cultural, social, moral, and psychic situation induced by slavery and its perduring legacy. Although there is no *normative* black experience, this distinction provides the basis for speaking of an *authoritative* way of understanding blackness, the black experience, being black, and black being as well as an *authentic* way of living black being and of being black. This theology will affirm and sustain black humanity and, at the same time, affirm the dignity and grandeur of *all human life* as it comes from the hands of God.

3. A Catholic theological mediation in African American perspective will strive to articulate and to mediate an understanding of the word of God from *within* and for the compound-complexity of black or African American culture. That theology will judge culture and consciousness by fidelity to full black human (i.e., religious, moral, intellectual, psychic, physical) development. That theology will not shirk engagement in a "radical cognitive therapy aimed at a basic liberation of all human subjects through a heightening of their awareness whereby they appropriate the imperatives of human freedom as dynamic orientations to be attentive, to be intelligent, to be reasonable, and to be loving."[90]

4. A Catholic theological mediation in African American perspective will neither reproduce, nor indigenize a theology emanating from the culture of other people of other times and other places. Such a theology will confront and lay bare not only deformations in culture and consciousness, but also deformations in the tradition—whether dogmatic or philosophical, liturgical or pastoral, historical or social. Such a theology will not blink when full light is shone on the black encounter with the Catholic proclamation of the Christian message. Thus, a Catholic theological mediation in African American perspective will aim for creative and autonomous thematization: one that recovers *from within* African American culture, the signs, symbols, and images of religious experience and consciousness; that expresses black peoples' peculiar saving encounter with the Triune God and that challenges black peoples' faith in relation to a praxis which measures itself by the praxis of Jesus; and that understands and responds aggressively to black peoples' complex historical, cultural, social (i.e., political, economic, and technological), and vital situation.[91] A Catholic theological mediation in African American perspective will confront and lay bare deformations in the tradition—whether dogmatic or juridical, liturgical or pastoral-practical, philosophical or existential. Further, a Catholic theological mediation in African American perspective will never embellish black peoples' encounter with the Catholic proclamation of the Christian message in the United States.

5. A Catholic theological mediation in African American perspective must take note of the presence of Jesus of Nazareth at the center of the earliest African American religious discourse. Certainly, a Christianity *without* Jesus of Nazareth is unthinkable, but any Christianity that fails to grasp the demand for the concrete ongoing historiciza-

tion of the vocation of Jesus, of his dynamic and saving message is patently unauthentic. The critical articulation of a christology which takes on the questions, strivings, aspirations, and tasks of the time of Jesus *as our own* and understands "that the gospel [does not furnish] us with specific, singular content, but with a model of self-restructuring in and by history," needs to, could, and must come from this perspective.[92] Such an undertaking would be precarious, but it would be a contribution of inestimable worth.

6. A Catholic theological mediation in African American perspective will prize interdisciplinarity. Adequate apprehension and understanding of the dense differentiated layers of the African, African American, Catholic *religious experience(s)* will require the collaborative work of theologians with biblical exegetes, anthropologists, geographers, linguists, ethnologists, musicologists, historians, art historians, historians of religions, cultural critics, literary critics, metaphysicians, ontologists, and philosophers. Adequate apprehension and understanding of the dense differentiated layers of *culture* will require the collaborative work of theologians with historians, cultural critics, musicologists, philosophers, and sociologists.

7. A Catholic theological mediation in African American perspective will valorize and link aesthetics and conceptual rigorousness. That theology will hold itself answerable to the three-fold criteria of orthodoxy, orthopraxy, and orthopathy that not only meet the normative canons of truth, but nourish the moral and existential, the social and historical, the personal and interpersonal, the affective and psychic.[93]

Conclusion

Some years ago, Dr. Jamie T. Phelps, O.P., called upon theologians to explore and employ African American experience as a source for Catholic theological reflection.[94] Such has been the aim of the three sections of this inquiry. In the first section, attention to the notions of conversion, foundations, and perspective focused on the theologian and the theologian's world. This provided a basis for the claim that foundations in theology is identical with the converted, self-appropriating theologian. Still, as I noted above, it is one thing to assert that foundations of a Catholic Theology in an African American perspective are rooted in the religious, moral, intellectual, and psychic conversions of the African American Catholic theologian; it

is quite another to draw out concretely the implications of that assertion. The explorations of the second section stand as a beginning in
this effort. First, I sketched out some of the implications of religious
conversion in *base-line religious consciousness* expressed as 'black religion'. Black religion is an historical phenomenon *neither* Protestant
nor Catholic, normatively centered in an African worldview, *even if*
the language of its expression and the symbols of its ritual are Christian in inspiration and in fact; *even* if the very features of the Christianity peculiar to the enslaved peoples masked their Africanity. Next,
I teased out and identified some incidents of masking that vibrant
Africanity: tracing sightings of the Kongo cosmogram in spirituals
and ceremonies of worship of the enslaved peoples; analyzing and
reflecting on the spiritual and two of its most intriguing and com-
pact themes—christology and anthropology. The purpose of this section was archaeological and, to some extent, pre-theological; but,
this excavation also had psychic consequences. Poignantly it disclosed
both continuity and discontinuity, order and fracture, gain and loss.
The third and final section offered seven characteristic features of an
African American Catholic theology.

My analysis has emphasized religious experience, because it insinuates the specifically theological principle, religious conversion. It has
emphasized religious consciousness, because religious consciousness
is *the* crucial mediation of African American personal and communal
transformation and self-transcendence and transformation. It has
relied on Bernard Lonergan's methodological proposals, because these
can provide a bridge for indigenous peoples, for Latino-, Celtic-,
Anglo-European Americans, for all women and men of good will
who want to understand African American efforts toward a Catholic
theological mediation from our perspective. Lonergan's framework
for collaborative creativity is a scaffold for initiating, developing, cor-
recting, and sustaining authentic religious, moral, intellectual, affective, and practical *cooperations*.

This is imperative: the future of Catholic Theology in the United
States depends upon our authentic collaborative creativity. Yet, authenticity, collaboration, correction, and creativity have conditions:
openness to religious, moral, intellectual, and psychic conversions;
regard for the mind of the "other" as instance of human mind; appropriation of one's own intelligence, reasonableness, and freedom;
apprehension and criticism of our individual and collective, personal

and social enmeshment in bias; desire and willingness for self-correc-
tion, for change, for transformation on individual and collective, personal and social planes; being willing to face basic issues without
yielding to individual temperament or personalistic evaluation.

This is imperative: the prospect that Catholic theology might live
in the twenty-first century as vividly and powerfully as it did in the
thirteenth depends, in no mean degree, on our foundations. Whether
or not, we—theologians, historians, ethicists, biblical exegetes, and
scholars—submit religious, moral, cognitive, and psychic consciousness to the explanatory task of theology. Whether or not, we ground
the theology we write in the discoveries that we have made and verified in the drive for truth and authentic direction in our own lives
and the life of the Christian community. Whether or not, we risk
"burst[ing] through the enchanted but vicious circle to deliver *the
real*" from confinement to mentality and custom, vocabulary and
system which twist and betray, stupefy and intimidate the gospel's
privileged and ineluctable power.[95]

Notes

[1] F. Eboussi Boulaga, *Christianity Without Fetishes: An African Critique and
Recapture of Christianity*, trans. Robert R. Barr (1981; Maryknoll, NY:
Orbis Books, 1984): 14.

[2] See Bernard Lonergan, "Dimensions of Meaning," in *Collection: Papers by
Bernard Lonergan*, ed. Frederick E. Crowe (Montreal: Palm Publishers,
1967): 252-67. See also, "The Transition from a Classicist World-View
to Historical-Mindedness," in *A Second Collection*, eds., William F. J.
Ryan and Bernard J. Tyrrell (Philadelphia: Westminster Press, 1974): 1-
10; "Theology in its New Context," ibid.:55-67; "Theology and Man's
Future," ibid.:135-48; "The Future of Christianity," ibid.:149-63; "Philosophy and Theology," ibid.:193-208; "Revolution in Catholic Theology," ibid.: 231-38.

[3] See Frederick E. Crowe, "Bernard Lonergan as Pastoral Theologian,"
Gregorianum 67 (1986): 451-70.

[4] Lonergan, "Theology in Its New Context," pp. 63, 67; ibid., "The Future
of Christianity," p. 161.

[5] Lonergan, *Method in Theology* (NY: Herder & Herder, 1972), pp. 20-25,
pp. 130-132, pp. 235-93.

[6] Lonergan, *Doctrinal Pluralism*, The 1971 Père Marquette Lecture (Milwaukee: Marquette University Press, 1971), p. 32.

[7] Lonergan, *Method in Theology*: 363, 271.

[8] See Charles H. Long, *Significations: Signs, Symbols, and Images in the Interpretation of Religion* (Philadelphia: Fortress Press, 1986): 9. Karla F. C.

Holloway, *Moorings and Metaphors: Figures of Culture and Gender in Black Women's Literature* (New Brunswick, NJ: Rutgers University Press, 1992): 13-14.

[9]Lonergan, *Method in Theology.* 20.

[10]Lonergan, *Method in Theology.* 20, 125-45.

[11]Ibid.: 245.

[12]Sterling Stuckey, *Slave Culture: Nationalist Theory and the Foundations of Black America* (NY: Oxford University Press, 1987); Abram Kardiner and Lionel Ovesey, *The Mark of Oppression: Explorations in the Personality of the American Negro* (1951; Cleveland: Meridian, 1962); Newbell Niles Puckett, *The Magic and Folk Beliefs of the Southern Negro* (1926; NY: Dover Publications, 1969); Lawrence Levine, *Black Culture and Black Consciousness: Afro-American Folk Thought from Slavery to Freedom* (NY: Oxford University Press, 1977); Mechal Sobel, *Trabelin' On: The Slave Journey to an Afro-Baptist Faith* (Princeton, NJ: Princeton University Press, 1979); Albert J. Raboteau, *Slave Religion: The 'Invisible Institution' in the Antebellum South*; Gayraud S. Wilmore, *Black Religion and Black Radicalism: An Interpretation of the Religious History of Afro-American People* (Maryknoll, NY: Orbis Books,1973; 2nd rev. ed. 1983), Cyprian Davis, *The History of Black Catholics in the United States* (NY: Crossroad, 1990).

[13]Lonergan treats the term *bias* with great precision: it is not to be confused with particular preference or tendency, or an inclination of temperament. Bias distorts and inhibits our conscious performance in everyday living by blinding our understanding. See Lonergan, *Insight, A Study of Human Understanding* (London: Longmans, Green and Company, 1957), Ch. 7.

[14]Lonergan, *Method in Theology.* 247.

[15]William R. Jones, *Is God A White Racist?: A Preamble to Black Theology* (Garden City, NY: Doubleday, 1973): 21-22.

[16]On Lonergan's account, basic conversion is *threefold*: religious, moral, and intellectual. Robert Doran extends and complements this basic pattern with a fourth—psychic conversion, which, in principle, is independent of the three specified by Lonergan, yet contributes radically to the task of sublation regarding the others. See Robert M. Doran, "The Theologian's Psyche: Notes Toward a Reconstruction of Depth Psychology," *Lonergan Workshop*, vol. 1, ed., Fred Lawrence (Missoula, MT: Scholars Press, 1978): 93-141; Idem., *Psychic Conversion and Theological Foundations: Toward a Reorientation of the Human Science* (Atlanta, GA: Scholars Press, 1981).

[17]Long, *Significations.* 8.

[18]Clifton H. Johnson, ed., *God Struck Me Dead: Voices of Ex-Slaves* (; Cleveland, OH: The Pilgrim Press, 1969;1993): 59-60. This paper makes use of three editions of this work, n.50, n.65. These editions vary (1) by scholarly introductions and essays and (2) by arrangement of material and the inclusion and/or exclusion of one or another narrative.

[19]Kimberly Rae Connor, *Conversions and Visions in the Writings of African-American Women* (Knoxville: University of Tennessee, 1994), p. 27.

[20]Ibid., p. 26.

[21]Lonergan, "The Subject," in *A Second Collection*: 77.

[22]See Cornel West, *Prophesy Deliverance! An Afro-American Revolutionary Christianity* (Philadelphia: Westminster Press, 1982): 47-65 and Susan Griffin, "Pornography and Silence," in her *Made From This Earth: An Anthology of Writings by Susan Griffin* (NY: Harper & Row, 1982): 110-60.

[23]Lonergan, *Method in Theology*: 238. Idem, "Cognitional Structure," in *Collection*: 221-39.

[24]William Edward Burghardt DuBois, The Souls of Black Folks (1903; NY: Fawcett Publications, Inc., 1961): 16-17.

[25]Doran, *Theology and the Dialectics of History* (Toronto: University of Toronto Press, 1990), p. 62.

[26]See Frantz Fanon, *Black Skins, White Masks*, trans. Charles Lamm Markmann (New York: Grove Press, 1967) and Lewis R. Gordon, *Bad Faith and Antiblack Racism* (Atlantic Highlands, NJ: Humanities Press, 1995).

[27]Lonergan, *Method in Theology*, pp. 267-68.

[28]Ibid., pp. 270, 13-25.

[29]Victor Turner, *Dramas, Fields, and Metaphors: Symbolic Action in Human Society* (Ithaca and London: Cornell University Press, 1974), pp. 67, 163.

[30]Clifford Geertz, *The Interpretation of Cultures: Selected Essays* (New York: Basic Books, 1973), p. 89.

[31]See Rudolf Otto, *The Idea of the Holy*, trans. John W. Harvey (Oxford: Oxford University press, 1958); Mircea Eliade, *The Sacred and the Profane: The Nature of Religion*, trans. Willard R. Trask (New York: Harcourt, Brace & World, 1959); idem, *The Myth of the Eternal Return*, trans. Willard R. Trask (New York: Pantheon Books, 1954).

[32]The notion of the existence of one supreme Deity and of lesser gods or divinities is common among many peoples of Africa. The supreme Deity is the source of power and authority within the pantheon of divinities or spirits. This belief is expressed exquisitely in the Yoruba proverb: "Be there one thousand four hundred divinities of the home; Be there one thousand two hundred divinities of the market place; Yet there is not one divinity to compare with Olódùmarè: Olódùmarè is the King Unique" (Cited in E. Bolaji Idowu, *Olódùmarè: God in Yoruba Belief* [Ikeja, Nigeria: Longman, 1962], p. 55).

[33]Idowu, *African Traditional Religions: A Definition* (Maryknoll, NY: Orbis Books, 1973; 1975), p. 184.

[34]John S. Mbiti, *African Religions and Philosophies* (London: Heinemann, 1969; 2nd ed.1989), pp., 3, 37, 58-73, 74-89.

[35]Jon Butler, *Awash in a Sea of Faith, Christianizing the American People* (Cambridge, Mass.: Harvard University Press, 1990), p. 130.

[36]See Melville J. Herskovits, *The Myth of the Negro Past* (Boston: Beacon Press, 1941; 1958); Janheienz Jahn, Muntu: *African Culture and the Western World* (New York: Grove Press, 1955; 1961; 1990); Robert Farris Thompson, *Flash of the Spirit: African and Afro-American Art and Philosophy* (New York: Random House/Vintage Books, 1984); idem., *African Art in Motion: Icon and Act* (Los Angles: University of California Press, 1974); Robert Farris Thompson and Joseph Cornet, *The Four Moments of the Sun: Kongo Art in Two Worlds* (Washington, D.C.: National Gallery of Art, 1981); Charles H. Long, *Significations* (op. cit.); Mechal Sobel, *Trabelin' On* (op. cit.); Martha Washington Creel, *"A Peculiar People": Slave Religion and Community-Culture Among the Gullahs* (New York: New York University Press, 1988).

[37]I have not worked this out fully, but I am posing a distinction between 'Black religion' and African American Christianity. While any attempt at periodization is only heuristic, there are questions to be answered (e.g., What is the relationship of the Christianitiy of the enslaved peoples to the Great Awakening?). See also, Sobel, *Trabelin' On*, pp. 38-39.

[38]Turner, *Dramas, Fields, and Metaphors*, pp. 67, 163.

[39]Sobel, *Trabelin' On*, pp. xxii-xxiv, 3-21.

[40]Long, "Structural Similarities and Dissimilarities in Black and African Theologies," *The Journal of Religious Thought*, vol. 32, no. 2 (Fall/Winter 1975): 14, 21; idem., *Significations*, p. 9.

[41]Theo Witvliet, *The Way of the Black Messiah: The Hermeneutical Challenge of Black Theology as a Theology of Liberation*, trans. John Bowden (Oak Park, IL: Meyer Stone Books, 1987), p. 184. This same point is made by Gayraud S. Wilmore, *Black Religion and Black Radicalism* (op. cit.), pp. 218-19, 223, 234.

[42]Philip Curtin estimates that "fully one-third of United States Blacks are of Kongo and Angolo ancestry," quoted in Robert Farris Thompson and Joseph Cornet, *The Four Moments of the Sun*, pp. 32, 27.

[43]Thompson, *Flash of the Spirit*, p. 106.

[44]Thompson and Cornet, *The Four Moments of the Sun*, 28.

[45]John M. Jantzen and Wyatt MacGaffey, *An Anthology of Kongo Religion: Primary Texts from Lower Zaire* (Lawrence: University of Kansas, 1974), p. 34.

[46]Thompson, *Flash of the Spirit*, p. 106-07.

[47]Sobel in *Trabelin On*'has documented the existence of at least thirty-seven independent Black churches between 1758 and 1822. See also Erskine Clarke, *Wrestlin' Jacob: A Portrait of Religion in the Old South* (Atlanta: John Knox Press, 1979), and Cyprian Davis, *The History of Black Catholics in the United States*.

[48]See Martha Washington Creel, "Community Regulation and Cultural Specialization in Gullah Folk Religion," 59-63, in *African American Christianity: Essays in History*, ed. Paul E. Johnson (Berkeley: University of California Press, 1994); cf., Raboteau, *Slave Religion*, pp. 43-92.

[49]See John W. Blassingame, *The Slave Community: Plantation Life in the Antebellum South* (New York: Oxford University Press, 1972; 1979), pp. 3-48; Eugene D. Genovese, *Roll, Jordon, Roll: The World the Slaves Made* (New York: Pantheon, 1974), pp., 161-279; and Lawrence Levine, *Black Culture and Black Consciousness: Afro-American Folk Thought from Slavery to Freedom* (New York: Oxford University Press, 1977), pp. 3-80.

[50]C. Johnson and A. P. Watson, eds., *God Struck Me Dead: Religious Conversion Experiences and Autobiographies of Ex-Slaves* (Philadelphia and New York: The Pilgrim Press, 1969), vii.

[51]Quoted in Stuckey, *Slave Culture*, p. 33; see also "Untitled Reports," Howard University Library, Washington, D.C., M248-M96. February 1974, quoted, in Harold Carter, *The Prayer Tradition of Black People* (Valley Forge: Judson Press, 1976), pp. 48-49.

[52]See John Lovell, Jr., *Black Song: The Forge and the Flame—The Story of How the Afro-American Spiritual Was Hammered Out* (1972; New York: Paragon, 1986), p. 401; see Mark Fisher, *Negro Slave Songs in the United States* (New York: Citadel Press, 1953).

[53]James Weldon Johnson and J. Rosamond Johnson, *The Books of American Negro Spirituals*, 2 vols (New York: Da Capo Press, Inc., 1925; 1926; 1969; 1989), pp. 11-12.

[54]Zora Neale Hurston, *The Sanctified Church* (Berkeley, CA: Turtle Island, 1983), p. 80.

[55]M. V. Bales, "Some Negro Folk Songs of Texas," p. 85, in *Follow De Drinkin' Gou'd*, ed., James Dobie (Austin: Texas Folklore Society, 1928).

[56]Quoted in Raboteau, *Slave Religion*, p. 246; cf., Hurston, *The Sanctified Church*, pp. 69-78.

[57]Raboteau, *Slave Religion*, pp. 244-245.

[58]Portia K. Maultsby, "Africanisms in African-American Music," p. 193, in *Africanisms in American Culture*, ed. Joseph E. Holloway (Bloomington: Indiana University Press, 1990).

[59]Clarence Jos. *Rivers, The Spirit in Worship* (Cincinnati: Stimuli, Inc., 1978), p. 199.

[60]Long, *Significations*, p. 7.

[61]Hurston, *The Sanctified Church*, p. 80.

[62]Raboteau, *Slave Religion*, p. 245.

[63]Ibid., pp. 70-71. The ring shout "lives" in the worship of African Americans living in the small islands off the coasts of Georgia and the Carolinas and in Brazil in the rituals of Candomblé, a 'new world' adaptation of the traditional religion of the West African Yoruba.

[64]Thompson, *Flash of the Spirit*, p. 110.

[65]Clifton Johnson, *God Struck Me Dead: Voices of Ex-Slaves*, p. 147; cf., Charles Johnson, ed. *God Struck Me Dead: Religious Conversion Experiences and Autobiographies of Ex-Slaves* (Nashville: Fisk University, 1945), p. 163, quoted in Thompson, *Face of the Gods: Art and Altars of Africa and the African Americas* (New York/Munich: The Museum of African Art/Prestel, 1993), p. 80.

[66]William J. Faulkner, *The Days When the Animals Talked: Black-American Folktales and How They Came to Be* (1977; Trenton, NJ: Africa World Press, 1993), pp. 56-57.

[67]Quoted in Thompson, *Flash of the Spirit*, p. 108.

[68]Ibid., p. 108.

[69]This is not to contest oral tradition as a primatial characteristic of the cultures of the peoples of Africa. However ideographic writing among the Ejagham people of southwestern Cameroon and southeastern Nigeria rebuts the myth of Africa as a continent without writing. See, Thompson, *Flash of the Spirit*, pp. 227-68; cp., V. Y. Mudimbe, *The Invention of Africa: Gnosis, Philosophy, and the Order of Knowledge* (Bloomington: Indiana University Press, 1988), and D. A. Masolo, *African Philosophy in Search of Identity* (Bloomington: Indiana University Press, 1994], pp. 241-45.

[70]Lovell, *Black Song: the Forge and the Flame*, p. 257; see Janet Duitsman Cornelius, *When I Can Read My Title Clear: Literacy, Slavery, and Religion in the Antebellum South* (Columbia, South Carolina: University of South Carolina Press, 1991).

[71]Vincent L. Wimbush, "The Bible and African Americans: An Outline of an Interpretative History," p. 87, in *Stony the Road We Trod: African American Biblical Interpretation*, ed., Cain Hope Felder (Minneapolis: Fortress Press, 1991).

[72]Paul Radin, "Status, Phantasy, and the Christian Dogma," p. v, in *God Struck Me Dead: Religious Conversion Experiences and Autobiographies of Ex-Slaves*, ed. Charles Johnson. In this introductory essay, Radin affirms what I had begun to think: "The ante-bellum Negro was not converted to God. He converted God to himself."

[73]Lovell, *Black Song: The Forge and the Flame*, p. 258.

[74]Ibid., pp. 260-61.

[75]This same point is made by both Arthur C. Jones, *Wade in the Water: The Wisdom of the Spirituals* (Maryknoll, NY: Orbis, 1993), pp. 69-71, and Lovell, *Black Song: The Forge and the Flame*, pp. 191-92.

[76]Creel, "Community Regulation and Cultural Specialization in Gullah Folk Religion," p. 51; for a similar account, see *Frederick Douglass: The Narrative and Selected Writings*, ed. Michael Meyer (New York: Random House/Modern Library College Edition, 1984), pp. 66-67.

[77]Lovell, *Black Song: The Forge and the Flame*, p. 191.

[78]Ibid., p. 192.

[79]*Narrative of the Life of Frederick Douglass an American Slave* (1845) pp. 28-29, quoted in Lovell, *Black Song: The Forge and the Flame*, p. 195.

[80]James H. Cone, *The Spirituals and the Blues* (1972; Maryknoll, NY: Orbis Books, 1991), p. 43.

[81]Cp., Henry Mitchell, *Black Belief* (San Francisco: Harper & Row, 1975), p. 120; Gayraud Wilmore, *Black Religion and Black Radicalism*, p. 217.

[82]See Roger D. Abrahams, *Singing the Master: The Emergence of African American Culture in the Plantation South* (New York: Pantheon Books,

1992), Idem, *Afro-American Folktales, Stories from Black Traditions in the New World* (New York: Pantheon Fairy Tale and Folklore Library, 1985); Edward C. L. Adams, ed., *Tales of the Congaree* (1927; Chapel Hill: University of North Carolina Press, 1987).

[83]Howard Thurman, *Deep River and The Negro Spiritual Speaks of Life and Death* (Indiana: Friends Untied Press, 1975), p. 16.

[84]Ernst Käsenann, *Jesus Means Freedom* (Phildelphia: Fortress Press, 1977).

[85]Blassingame, ed., *Slave Testimony: Two Centuries of Letters, Speeches, Interviews, and Autobiographies* (Baton Rouge: Louisiana State University Press, 1977), p. 220.

[86]Cone, *Spirituals and the Blues*, p. 49

[87]Lovell, *Black Song: The Forge and the Flame*, p. 189.

[88]Theo Witvliet, *The Way of the Black Messiah* (op. cit.), p. 203.

[89]Lonergan, "Theology in its New Context," pp. 62-63.

[90]Matthew L. Lamb, *Solidarity with Victims: Toward a Theology of Social Transformation* (New York: Crossroad, 1982), p. 85.

[91]Cf. Boulaga, *Christianity Without Fetishes*, Chapters 8-11.

[92]Ibid., p. 86.

[93]Jamie T. Phelps, O.P., "The Sources of Theology: African-American Catholic Experience in the United States," (paper presented at the annual meeting of the Catholic Theological Society of America, Toronto, Ontario, Canada, June 1988), typescript, pp. 7-8.

[94]Ibid.

[95]Boulaga, *Christianity Without Fetishes*, p. 216.

Appendix 1
Foundations for Catholic Theology in an African American Perspective: The Bibliographic Essay

M. Shawn Copeland, Ph.D.
Marquette University: Milwaukee, Wisconsin

More than twenty-five years ago, the noted historian Robert T. Handy criticized American church historiography for its incidental and casual treatment of the history of Christianity among black people and the reduction of that history to "a 'special topic' to be treated in connection with certain definite crises or to be handled by those with a particular interest in that subject."[1] While Handy concluded his bibliographic essay by exhorting scholars to attend to this neglected field, he could not have anticipated the explosion of research and publication that occurred in the late 1960s and 1970s and that accorded mainstream legitimation to the study of the black experience.

The results of this explosion have consolidated in paradigm change, not only in the *content* and *method* of the study of black culture and history, but also in theology. The new "Black Studies" set the academic and cultural trajectory for change in content and method in humanist studies in the United States, for example, in history, literature, the arts, philosophy, theology, and religion. As black studies became increasingly recursive, it became increasingly African-centered, thus, a further change in paradigm—*Afrocentricism*. Despite deeply controversial, conflictual, and polemical usage, most basically Afrocentrism may be defined as a point of departure for asking and answering questions that places "African ideals at the center of any analysis that involves African culture and behavior."[2]

Black studies cleared intellectual ground for a distinctive and critical form of reflection on and from within the horizon of Christian faith. This distinctive and critical form of reflection took as its point of departure the history of cultural, psychic, moral, social (i.e., political, economic, technological), and legal oppression of black hu-

man beings and questioned the religious and theological legitimation of that oppression and its consequences for a life of faith among
black women and men as well a life of critically questioning that
faith and its contradictory impulses of subjugation and liberation.

This chapter, "Foundations for Catholic Theology in an African
American Perspective," presupposes this paradigm change in content
and method, even if it interprets these changes *critically* and *differently*. That is to say, it presupposes black studies and Afrocentricism;
it also presupposes black theology and its grasp and interpretation of
the revelatory, prophetic, sacrificial, emancipatory, and liberatory
modes of black religion and of African American Christianity. This
essay identifies some of the materials researched and referenced in
the chapter as well as addresses basic research for teaching. Apropos
of this latter, it distinguishes seven basic areas of research for teaching
the African American religious experience.

First, any research on the African American religious experience is
obliged to address the historic involuntary presence of peoples of
African descent in the United States. Peter J. *Parish in Slavery: History and Historians* (New York: Icon Editions/Harper and Row, 1989)
presents an excellent historiographic essay. Large philosophical studies of slavery include, Frank Tannenbaum, *Slave and Citizen* (1946;
Boston: Beacon Press, 1992); David Brian Davis, *The Problem of Slavery in Western Culture* (Ithaca, NY: Cornell University Press, 1966);
idem, *The Problem of Slavery in the Age of Revolution, 1770-1823*
(Ithaca, NY: Cornell University Press, 1975); and Orlando Patterson,
Slavery and Social Death, A Comparative Study (Cambridge, MA:
Harvard University Press, 1982).

The first major scholarly study of slavery was that by Ulrich B.
Phillips, *American Negro Slavery: A Survey of the Supply, Employment,
and Control of Negro Labor as Determined by the Plantation Regime*
(1918; reprint, Baton Rouge, LA: Louisiana State University Press,
1966). Phillips was generally sympathetic to the practices of slavery
in the South and placed white supremacy at the center of Southern
history. Nearly forty years later, Kenneth M. Stampp, *The Peculiar
Institution: Slavery in the Ante-bellum South* (New York: Vintage Books,
1956) methodically challenged and, inevitably, displaced Phillips's
analysis.

Studies treating the organization, economy, efficiency, and effects
of the Atlantic slave trade include Daniel P. Mannix and Malcolm

Cowley, *Black Cargoes: A History of the Atlantic Slave Trade* (New York: Penguin Books, 1962); Philip Curtin, *The Atlantic Slave Trade: A Census* (Madison: University of Wisconsin Press, 1969); and Peter Kolchin, *American Slavery 1619-1877* (New York: Hill and Wang, 1993). Eugene Genovese, *The Political Economy of Slavery: Studies in the Society of the Slave South* (New York: Pantheon Books, 1965) argued that the slavery set the South apart from the remainder of the United States. The critique of this view, namely that ante-bellum slavery was a Southern variant of American capitalism is argued by James Oakes, *The Ruling Race: A History of American Slaveholders* (New York: Random House, 1983), although Oakes seems to have retreated from this position in *Slavery and Freedom: An Interpretation of the Old South* (New York: Random House, 1990).

Second, research is needed on the cultural complexities from which the Africans were forcibly removed: languages; customs and traditions; male and female secret societies which regulated moral and social life; divisions of labor, roles, and functions constituting kin and social groups; loci of moral authority; the exercise and transmission of political and social power; the enforcement of secrets and taboos; incarnate and expressed meanings of beauty and deformity, satire and folly, value and disvalue, good and evil, truth and falsehood. Two important introductory studies are those by Roger Bastide, *African Civilizations in the New World* (New York: Harper & Row, 1971) and Cheikh Anta Diop, *The African Origin of Civilization, Myth or Reality,* trans. and ed., Mercer Cook (1955; 1967; New York and Westport, CT: Lawrence Hill, 1974). The discussion on the relation and place of African civilizations to the West has benefited from Martin Bernal, *Black Athena: The Afroasiatic Roots of Classical Civilization,* 2 vols (New Brunswick, NJ: Rutgers University Press, 1987, 1991). In Muntu: *African Culture and the Western World* (1955; 1961; New York: Grove Press, 1990) Janheinz Jahn pioneered scholarly engagement with African cultures on their own terms. The field work, aesthetic and philosophical analysis of art historians has been especially crucial in negotiating Africanisms in African American customs and mores. Especially helpful studies are those by Robert Farris Thompson, *Flash of the Spirit: African and Afro-American Art and Philosophy* (New York: Random House/Vintage Books, 1984), idem., *African Art in Motion: Icon and Act* (Los Angles: University of California Press, 1974), Robert Farris Thompson and Joseph Cornet, *The Four Moments of the Sun: Kongo Art in Two Worlds* (Washington, D.C.: National Gallery of Art, 1981).

The study of 'Africanisms'—persistent, identifiable remnants of language, custom, ritual, aesthetic meaning and practice that carried as well as blended or fused with various meanings, practices, and values of various ethnic-cultural groups from whom the enslaved peoples came—constitutes a crucial and controversial area of inquiry and research. The foremost proponent of the retention of Africanisms in the creation of African American culture was the anthropologist Melville J. Herskovits, whose thesis is presented in *The Myth of the Negro Past* (1941; Boston: Beacon Press, 1958). Herskovits' work followed in the wake of Newbell Niles Puckett's, *Folk Beliefs of the Southern Negro* (Chapel Hill: University of North Carolina Press, 1926) and Carter G. Woodson's, *The African Background Outlined* (1936; New York: Negro University Press, 1968). Herskovits' work presented a sophisticated, nuanced, fine-grained analysis and shared Woodson's scholarly passion for clarifying the historical and cultural record about Blacks. Herskovits extended the claim for the retention of Africanisms, arguing that despite differences among numerous ethnic-linguistic groups, West Africa formed a kind of cultural whole; that despite linguistic, social, and particular cultural differences, that the enslaved peoples retained, shared, and adapted cultural mores and practices; and that African cultural elements are persistently discernible in contemporary expressions of African American culture, especially in religious rituals and practices. This position was contested by sociologist E. Franklin Frazier. In *The Negro Church in America* (New York: Schocken, 1964), Frazier insisted that slavery destroyed the cultural heritage and traditions of the enslaved peoples and that African American culture evolved quite apart from African elements and influence. Scholars continue to debate the status and scope of retentions, but Herskovits' thesis holds the field. For a most important collection of essays regarding question and advancing Herskovits' thesis, see Joseph E. Holloway, ed., *Africanisms in American Culture* (Bloomington: Indiana University Press, 1990); Sterling Stuckey, *Slave Culture: Nationalist Theory and the Foundations of Black America* (New York: Oxford University Press, 1987), especially, pp. 3-97; Gayl Jones, *Liberating Voices: Oral Tradition in African American Literature* (New York: Penguin, 1991), and Sidney W. Mintz and Richard Price, *The Birth of African American Culture: An Anthropo-*

logical Perspective (1976; Boston: Beacon Press, 1992).

The elements of religio-cultural life that the enslaved Africans blended, fused, preserved and transmitted, as well as the subtle, subversive relation of those elements and their reconfigured appearance in 'Black religion,' and the enslaved peoples (revelatory) reception and transmission of African American Christianity constitute a *third* crucial area for research. Key issues include the Negro Spirituals; the creation of a 'slave bible'; religious experience and religious consciousness (conversion, visions, and spirit possession).

For some comparative discussions relating traditional African beliefs and those of Christianity see John S. Mbiti, *God in Africa* (London: SPCK, 1970); idem, *African Religions and Philosophy* (1969; Oxford: Heinemann, 1988); Okot p'Bitek, *African Religions in Western Scholarship* (Nairobi: East African Literature Bureau, 1970); Dominique Zahan, *The Religion, Spirituality, and Thought of Traditional Africa*, trans. Kate Ezra and Lawrence M. Martin (Chicago: University of Chicago Press, 1979); and E. Bojali Idowu, *African Traditional Religion: A Definition* (Maryknoll, NY: Orbis Books, 1975).

The foremost treatment of the "Negro spiritual" is provided by John Lovell, Jr., *Black Song: The Forge and the Flame—The Story of How the Afro-American Spiritual Was Hammered Out* (1972; New York: Paragon, 1986). Other important treatments of the spirituals and their aesthetic power and significance in African American music include Miles Mark Fisher, *Negro Slave Songs in the United States* (New York: Citadel Press, 1953; Howard Thurman, *Deep River and The Negro Spiritual Speaks of Life and Death* (Indiana: Friends Untied Press, 1975); LeRoi Jones, *Blues People: The Negro Experience in White America and the Music That Developed from It* (New York: William Morrow, 1963); and Eileen Southern, *The Music of Black Americans: A History* (New York: W. W. Norton, 2nd ed. 1983). Theological treatments of the spirituals are presented by James H. Cone, *The Spirituals and the Blues: An Interpretation* (Westport, CT: Greenwood Press, 1972) and Jon Michael Spencer, *Protest and Praise: Sacred Music of Black Religion* (Minneapolis: Fortress Press, 1990).

African American spirituals are included in *Lead Me, Guide Me: The African American Catholic Hymnal* (Chicago: G. I. A. Publications, 1987). The hymnal was made possible not only by the renewal of the Roman liturgy, but by the pioneering work of African American Roman Catholic priest and liturgist Clarence Joseph Rivers who first moved and inspired us to bring the whole of our artistic and cultural genius to Catholic worship, and by the practical and unflagging efforts of the late Archbishop James Patterson Lyke, O.F.M. The hymnal includes spirituals of praise, adoration, and thanksgiving, such as "My Lord! What a Morning," "I Will Trust in the Lord," "I've Just Come from the Fountain," "I Love the Lord," "Is There Anybody Here Who Loves My Jesus," "Deep River," and "I'm So Glad, Jesus Lifted Me." There are spirituals of prophecy and protest, such as "Glory, Glory Hallelujah, I Feel Better Since I Laid My Burden Down," "I Shall Not Be Moved," "Free at Last," "Oh, Freedom," "Woke Up This Morning, With My Mind Stayed on Jesus," "We've Come a Long Way Lord," "Go Down, Moses." There are spirituals of petition and prayer, such as "I Want Jesus to Walk With Me," "Lord, Make Me More Holy," "Standin' in the Need of Prayer," "Lord, I Want to Be a Christian," and "Cert'nly Lord." And there are spirituals of dense and dark luminosity and mystery, such as "Ezekiel Saw the Wheel," "Done Made My Vow to the Lord," "Ah Tol' Jesus It Would Be All Right If He Changed My Name," "Fix Me, Jesus," "I Know the Lord's Laid His Hands on Me," "Give Me Jesus."

Stony the Road We Trod: African American Biblical Interpretation (Minneapolis: Fortress Press, 1991) edited by Cain Hope Felder makes a significant contribution to our understanding of the enslaved peoples' encounter with the Hebrew and Christian Scriptures. In a chapter from that collection, "African American Women and the Bible," Renita J. Weems writes, "since slave communities were illiterate, they were, therefore, without allegiance to any official text, translation, or interpretation; hence once they heard biblical passages read and interpreted to them, they in turn were free to remember and repeat in accordance with their own interests and tastes.... [F]or those raised within an aural culture retelling the Bible became one hermeneutical strategy, and resistance to the Bible, or portions of it, would become another," (in *Stony the Road We Trod*, p. 61). This same issue is treated by sociologist of religion, Cheryl Townsend Gilkes who makes the claim that the "oral text" is the creation of an African American biblical tradition (cf. "Mother to the Motherless, Father to the Fatherless: Power, Gender and Community in an Afro-Centric Biblical Tradition," *Semeia* 47 1989). Gilkes argues that the composition of the "oral text" was a communal process: members of the enslaved community extracted from the preached or spoken (i.e., written) text what the community apprehended and judged as life affirming; this became normative for its survival, existence, and life. These extractions of selections were apprehended and judged as the true word of God in the Bible. These phrases or stories or descriptions of personalities were handed down from generation to generation in story and song and moral prescription. Another useful work is *Experience and Tradition: A Primer in Black Biblical Hermeneutics* (Nashville: Abingdon Press, 1990) by Stephen Breck Reid.

While some scholars may disagree with Albert J. Raboteau regarding "the death of the Africans gods," his *Slave Religion: The "Invisible Institution" in the Ante-bellum South* (New York: Oxford University Press, 1978) inaugurated the type of interdisciplinary synthetic study that has come to characterize the current discussion of Africanisms in the religious life and consciousness of the enslaved African peoples. Two other studies in this area include, Mechal Sobel, *Trabelin' On: The Slave Journey to an Afro-Baptist Faith* (Princeton, NJ: Princeton University Press, 1979) and Martha Washington Creel, *"A Peculiar People": Slave Religion and Community-Culture Among the Gullahs* (New York: New York University Press, 1988).

The following studies have established a shift within black theology: Dwight N. Hopkins and George Cummings, ed., *Cut Loose Your Stammering Tongue: Black Theology in the Slave Narratives* (Maryknoll, NY: Orbis Books, 1991); Dwight N. Hopkins, *Shoes That Fit Our Feet: Sources for a Constructive Black Theology* (Maryknoll, NY: Orbis Books, 1993); Riggins Earl, Jr., *Dark Symbols, Obscure Signs: God, Self, and Community in the Slave Mind* (Maryknoll, NY: Orbis Books, 1993); Theophus H. Smith, *Conjuring Culture: Biblical Formations of Black America* (New York: Oxford University Press, 1994). These works decenter racial critique, without abandoning it; and center the slave narratives as the crucial source in understanding the mentality and practices of the enslaved peoples.

A *fourth* area wherein research is needed regards the cultural, social (i.e., political, economic, and technological) lives of the enslaved African peoples. Eye-witness accounts are invaluable. For some excellent collections, see Herbert Aptheker, ed., *A Documentary History of the Negro People in the United States,* 7 vols. (Secaucus, NJ: Carol Publishing Group/Citadel Press, 1993, 1994); John W. Blassingame, ed., *Slave Testimony: Two Centuries of Letters, Speeches, Interviews, and Autobiographies* (Baton Rouge: Louisiana State University Press, 1977);

James Mellon, ed., *Bullwhip Days: The Slaves Remember, An Oral History* (New York: Avon Books, 1988); and Ira Berlin, Barbara J. Fields, et al., eds., *Free at Last: A Documentary History of Slavery, Freedom, and the Civil War* (New York: The New Press, 1992). *From Slavery to Freedom: A History of African Americans,* 7th rev. ed. (New York: Knopf, 1994) by John Hope Franklin and Alfred A. Moss is not only 'the standard' one-volume history, it is also accessible and easily available. More focused studies are presented by John W. Blassingame, *The Slave Community: Plantation Life in the Ante-bellum South* (1972; New York: Oxford University Press, 1979); Eugene D. Genovese, *Roll, Jordan, Roll: The World the Slaves Made* (New York: Pantheon Books, 1974); W. E. B. DuBois, *Black Reconstruction in America: An Essay Toward a History of the Part which Black Folk Played in the Attempt to Reconstruct Democracy in America, 1860-1880* (1935; New York: Atheneum/Macmillan, 1969); Leon Litwack, *Been in the Storm So Long: The Aftermath of Slavery* (1979; New York: Random House/Vintage Books, 1980).

The angular position of women within an oppressed community has not gone unnoticed. Historian Gerda Lerner edited *Black Women in White America: A Documentary History* (New York: Pantheon Books, 1972) which challenged us to listen to the voices of enslaved black women and *Ar'n't I a Woman? Female Slaves in the Plantation South* (New York: W. W. Norton, 1985) by Deborah Gray White added to an understanding of the work of women on plantations. These appeared well before the multivolume *The Schomburg Library of Nineteenth-Century Black Women Writers* (New York: Oxford University Press, 1988), edited by Henry Louis Gates, Jr.

An understanding of the religious, psychic, cultural, social (i.e., political, economic, and technological) world of the planter class is a *fifth* area of research. Conspicuous topics include the Christianity of the plantation, the economic impact of the Atlantic slave trade, the formation of political decisions regarding the citizen and the slave, the psychic condition of the slave owner. An anthology of proslavery writings is Drew Gilpin Faust, ed., *The Ideology of Slavery: Proslavery Thought in the Ante-bellum South, 1830-1860* (Baton Rouge, LA: Louisiana State University Press, 1981). Other trenchant studies include, Winthrop D. Jordan, *White Over Black: American Attitudes Toward the Negro, 1550-1812* (1968; New York: W. W. Norton, 1977); Eugene D. Genovese, *The World the Slaveholders Made* (1969; New

York: Random House/Vintage Books, 1971); George M. Frederickson, *The Black Image in the White Mind: The Debate on Afro-American Character and Destiny, 1817-1914* (Middletown, CT: Wesleyan University Press, 1971); and Forrest G. Wood, *The Arrogance of Faith: Christianity and Race in America from the Colonial Era to the Twentieth Century* (Boston: Northeastern University Press, 1990).

Sixth, study of the cultural and societal formation of the Catholic Church in the United States is also essential. Jay Dolan, *The American Catholic Experience: A History from Colonial Times to the Present* (Garden City: Doubleday, 1985) limits the African American contact with the Catholic Church to the 1960s. In doing so, Dolan unwittingly affirms E. Franklin Frazier's elision between black upward mobility and membership in the Roman Catholic Church. James Hennesey in *American Catholics: A History of the Roman Catholic Community in the United States* (New York: Oxford University Press, 1981) not only counters that stereotype in a social history of the U.S. Catholic Church, but advances a thesis that disputes the dominant historical interpretation of the Catholic Church in the United States as an 'immigrant church.'

Seventh, research treating the Church's encounter, ministry, and engagement with the enslaved African peoples and their posterity is needed. Of course, Cyprian Davis, *The History of Black Catholics in the United States* (New York: Crossroad Publishing, 1990) and Gayraud S. Wilmore, *Black Religion and Black Radicalism: An Interpretation of the Religious History of Afro-American People* (Maryknoll, NY: Orbis Books, 2nd rev. ed. 1983) are indispensable. Two informative and recent collections are Randall M. Miller and Jon L. Wakelyn, *Catholics in the Old South: Essays on Church and Culture* (Macon: Mercer University Press, 1983) and Kenneth J. Zanca, ed., *American Catholics and Slavery, 1789-1866* (Lanham, MD: University Press of America, 1994). Earlier studies investigating ecclesiastical attitudes include, Madeleine Hooke Rice, *American Catholic Opinion in the Slavery Controversy* (New York: Columbia University Press, 1944), William A. Osborne, *Segregated Covenant: Race Relations and American Catholics* (New York: Herder & Herder, 1967). Two dissertations of note: Edward J. Misch, "The American Bishops and the Negro from the Civil War to the Third Plenary Council of Baltimore 1865-1884" (Ph.D. dissertation, Pontifical Gregorian University, 1968) and Jamie T. Phelps, OP, "The Mission Ecclesiology of John

R. Slattery: A Study of African-American Mission of the Catholic Church in the Nineteenth Century," (Ph.D. dissertation, The Catholic University of America, 1989). In *Desegregating the Altar: The Josephites and the Struggle for Black Priests, 1871-1960* (Baton Rouge, LA: Louisiana State University Press, 1990), Stephen J. Ochs, while studying the changing views of the Josephites (and a few other religious orders) on the 'suitability' of black men for Roman Catholic priesthood, provides a careful and nuanced presentation of Roman Catholic accommodation to the custom and culture of slavery and segregation in the United States.

The Secretariat for African American Catholics, under the sponsorship of the United States Catholic Conference (USCC), the administrative arm of the National Conference of Catholic Bishops (NCCB), has taken responsibility to support sound and informative publications on the African-American Catholic experience which are accessible to a general reading audience. One such project is entitled *Many Rains Ago: A Historical and Theological Reflection on the Role of the Episcopate in the Evangelization of African American Catholics* (Washington, D.C.: USCC, 1990). Finally Christopher J. Kauffman, editor of the *U.S. Catholic Historian* has devoted three issues of that journal to the Black Catholic Experience, volume 5, number 1 (1986) and volume 7, numbers 2 and 3 (1988) volume 12, number 1 (1994).

Notes

[1] Robert T. Handy, "Negro Christianity and American Church Historiography," p. 91, in *Reinterpretation in American Church History*, vol. 5, *Essays in Divinity*, ed. J. C. Brauer (Chicago: University of Chicago Press, 1968); cf. August Meier and Elliot Rudwick, *Black History and the Historical Profession, 1915-1980* (Urbana and Chicago: University of Illinois Press, 1986).

[2] Molefi Kete Asante, *The Afrocentric Idea* (Philadelphia: Temple University Press, 1987), p. 86.

Appendix 2
The Sources of Theology: African-American Catholic Experience in the United States[1]

Jamie T. Phelps, O.P.
Catholic Theological Union: Chicago, Illinois

Introduction

The development of an American Catholic Theology would not be complete if we in the United States omitted the life contributions coming from our sisters and brothers who were born and raised in Canada, Central America, Latin America, the Caribbean, etc. But it would be equally incomplete if those of us who claim the United States of America as home were to omit the life and contributions of people of Color in our midst. The United States volume of the American Catholic Theology Series would be incomplete without chapters specifically reflecting the theological perspectives of Euro-Americans, Native-Americans, Asian-Americans, Hispanic-Americans and African-Americans.

As a theologian of African-American ancestry, culture and conscious identity, one of my theological birth rights and privileges is to participate in the theological interpretation of African-American life in all its rich complexity and diversity. Like Alice Walker, I believe that the truth about any subject only comes when all the sides of the story are put together, and all their different meanings make one new one. Each writer writes the missing parts to the others writer's story. And the whole story is what I'm after.[2]

For believers, the whole story is God's story—the story of a saving history. If we theologians are after the whole story of God's identity and action in history, we must discover God's revelation, as it is alive in the lives of all members of the human community. Otherwise we work from the distorted perspective of half-knowledge and partial truth. Just as we are beginning to emphasize new aspects of God's identity and revelation by the insights of black Protestant theology, liberation theology and feminist theology we must similarly explore the unique aspects of God's identity and revelation as experienced by other races and cultures within and beyond our Christian traditions.

Three questions can be asked of Black-Catholic Theology. What are its sources? What sources are shared with and distinct from Black-Theology in general? What can be said of the method and criteria of truth for Black-Catholic theology? But a prior question must be asked concerning the community from which this theology arises—What is the African-American Catholic Community?

Statistics

The number of African-American Catholics in the United States is currently estimated at two million. They are culturally and economically diverse. Many are middle class but like all African-Americans a large portion are economically poor. These latter are among the homeless, the unemployed, the uneducated and undereducated masses who do not have access to quality health care.[3] This environmental poverty however is not a poverty of intelligence nor inability to be self-directed, self-determined and creative. African-Americans who are poor possess an enormous creative ability for survival. This ability includes resourcefulness, sensitivity and respect for truthfulness, integrity, authenticity and justice. All too often ministers who serve in African-American Catholic parishes underestimate the intellectual keenness, spiritual depth and creative ability of their parishioners and prefer to develop relationships of dependence rather than collaboration.

African-American Catholics participate in three distinct but overlapping worlds of experience. At their core, consciously or unconsciously they are an African People, by birth and formal education they &e American, by choice they have been baptized and bathe themselves in the waters of Catholic theological tradition, religious ritual, and practices. There are rich and diverse mixtures of these three cultures in the life of African-American Catholics, which are not easily translated into a single descriptive stereotype.

African-American Catholic Diversity: Three Identifiable Groups

Though they do not embrace the entire complex of African American Catholics, three major African American Catholic subgroups groups are observable. The groups themselves are comprised of both cradle Catholics, including Creoles, and converts. The first group, of African-American Catholics, stresses its Catholic identity and maintains an undaunted loyalty to a reified Catholic heritage which was learned in the pre-Vatican II church.

This group articulates a concept of universality which is identified with a mythic uniformity and denies the legitimacy of pluralism or cultural diversity within the context of universality. Such Catholics were formed in the pre-Vatican II church and have not been exposed to or accepted any significant education regarding the insights of the Second Vatican Council which called for a transformation of church life and theological reformulation and development in some areas of understanding. This group generally resents being identified as "Black-Catholic and prefer worship and parish styles of organization which is priest centered and which they deem to be "traditional." Generally they view religion as a private affair but are moved to engage in acts of charity when confronted by human need. Such Catholics represent the deep desire of Black Catholics to be included within the mainstream of the Catholic Church. The psyche of many of these Catholics has not been able to forget that period in African-American life when "black" was the dominant culture's signal word for exclusion and mistreatment. Nor can they forget the negative attitudes of some Catholics both black and white, toward the rituals and music of the traditional Black Protestant Churches from which many of them had convened. Many came to the Catholic Church to forsake these emotionally expressive forms of worship of their birth churches and sought the quiet intellectual approach characteristic of the pre-Vatican Church.

A second identifiable group of African-American Catholics stresses their African and African-American heritage and consciously strive to find expression of this core identity in the context of their worship. This group generally prefers a " family" or community-centered worship style which integrates symbols and music from African and African-American traditions homilies that touch the pulse of African-American life as an oppressed but hopeful community. Since African-American tradition respects the role of minister as community leader; the priest is respected as a spiritual leader who aids the church community in organizing itself to address the spiritual and social needs of its extended families and all who live within the parish boundaries or who seek help from the church community. This groups consciousness resonates with the notion of church as the "People of God" found in and the need for cultural adaptation found in several documents from the Second Vatican Council notably, *Lumen Gentium, Ad Gentes and Gaudium et Spes.*

The third group maintains a clear African-American consciousness and commitment to the African-American community. However, it also focuses some of its intention on integrating its cultural heritage and consciousness into the mainstream of American-Catholicism. It struggles to articulate itself as a legitimate and unique form of Catholicism which is both Black and American. This latter group stresses the ideals of a re-born Americanism i.e. an egalitarian church in which the democratic ideal of the American society is historically manifest as a multi-cultural reality. This groups' major concern is the transformation of the local parish and the local church (diocese) and ultimately the United States into microcosm of the Kingdom of God which resembles the democratic ideal in which persons of diverse ethnic, racial, cultural and class backgrounds will find welcome. The members of this group share the worship, parish and leadership preferences of the second but are more open to a multi-cultural parish which has developed worship styles which use symbols, music, and homilies which express a consciousness of the multi-racial and multi-cultural reality of the human community.[4] This groups embodies a cultural interpretation of "communion ecclesiology" which undergirds all of the council documents i.e. the unity of the community born of the Spirit must find expression in the concrete unity of diverse cultures and local churches without denying their diversity or particularity.

This three-fold description does not exhaust the complexity of the two million African American Catholics within the United States since it is most applicable to native born African-Americans. Many Black-Catholic parishes have African-American Catholics reflecting all three perspectives, while individual Black-Catholics may experience transition from one perspective to another. Another significant factor affecting the African-American Catholic Community is that its population has been increased by recent African refuges and im-

migrants from Ethiopia, Eritrea, Haiti, Ghana, Nigeria, the West
Indians, the Virgin Islands, Cuba, Panama and other African coun-
tries and African-base. cultures throughout the world. One must keep
the cultural and economic complexity of African-American Catholics in mind when one embarks upon a search for the sources of
American Black-Catholic theology.

Sources for Black Catholic Theology in the United States

The two major sources of Black-Catholic theology are the Black
Experience (history life and culture) and Tradition (Sacred Scripture
and the Roman Catholic dogmatic tradition) When one asserts that
the primary source of an American Black-Catholic theology is the
collective experience of African-Americans and African-American
Catholics as reflected in their history and contemporary life. On. is
speaking of a complex array of individual and collective experiences
of members whose diverse experience find a common ground in a
paradigmatic event in United States History—the Civil War of 1861-
1865. Like the Old Testament Exodus event, the Civil War posed the
question of the freedom of diverse groups of oppressed slaves forged
into a single identity by the crucible of slavery—the African-American. Although all Blacks in the United States are not descendants of
nineteenth century slaves, all visible Blacks are subjected to racism
predicated on the dominant culture's continued "collective uncon-
scious" belief that most Blacks are intellectually, culturally and morally inferior to whites. This belief is still prevalent in the United States'
Catholic Church and society. Unable to maintain Blacks in subjugation, the nation first developed elaborate systems of segregation supported by political legislation and the churches. When segregation
was successfully challenged by the Civil Rights Movement of the nine-
teen sixties segregation yielded to the marginalization of Blacks by
attitudes of indifference and the debilitating but silent virus of structured institutional racism which had infected the nation since its
birth.

Edward K. Braxton has repeatedly noted the marginality of African-American Catholics within the Black-Community and the Catholic Community of the United States. Black Protestants often question the authenticity of the African-American Catholics' "blackness"
while White Catholics doubt their "catholicity." As a consequence
the thoughts, opinions and contributions of African American Catho-

lics are minimized or ignored by both groups. This marginality, however, provides a unique and critical viewpoint from which to start an original theological synthesis which, in fact, has already begun. Ten years ago, the National Black Catholic Clergy Caucus, supported Fr. Thaddeus Posey's, proposal to convene the First Black Catholic Theological Symposium.[5] In the proceedings from that conference, Joseph R. Nearon quoted his own article published in the CTSA proceedings of June, 1975. He outlined the twofold objective of Black Theology within the context of the Roman Catholic Tradition. "Black Theology may seek to give a black articulation of the Catholic faith. Secondly it may strive to give a Christian interpretation of the black experience."[6]

Nearon's objective was affirmed by the conference presenters whose papers were solicited with the request that the author use one of two starting points, the Christian traditions as contained in Scripture and Dogmatic formulations of the church and the Black experience. From its formal beginning then, Black-Catholic Theology has articulated a two-source starting point: Black experience and Catholic tradition. A review of the footnotes of the papers presented affirm this two-source supposition.

Black-Catholic Theology and Black Theology.[7]

Black theology was born in the heart of the Black Church. Until recently, the designation "Black Church" represented the totality of the traditional Black Churches in the United States which had originated as a consequence of the black memberships rejection of the racism and second-class citizenship they were relegated to in the mainline Protestant denominations, Baptist, Methodists etc. and those which had roots in the slave quarters and fields.[8] However there is increasing recognition that Blacks in predominately white Churches in the United States (e.g., Catholic, Presbyterian etc.) are indeed members of the Black Church insofar as they share the same social-cultural and spiritual heritage of Black people although the worship styles and organizational polity of their denominations have not generally reflected this reality.

African-American Catholics who have reclaimed their black heritage acknowledge the same social history and culture of other African-Americans in the United States. In seeking to articulate the Black experience in America they have recourse to the same history, and

African cultural roots. The knowledge collected regarding the psychological, cultural and historical distinctiveness of African-Americans apply equally to Protestants, Catholics, Muslims, Jewish and unchurched Blacks.[9] The African-American Catholic heritage found among Creole Catholics in the South and Southwest manifest a distinct French-African blend at the level of popular religion. The African appropriation of Catholicism which lies at the heart of the Black-Catholic psyche has not always been explicit but is nonetheless present. The all-pervasive consciousness of God's presence (contemplative posture) and the values of human universality, love for all creation, the primary value of interpersonal relationships and commitment to justice and liberation which arise from this primary consciousness are key themes which are reflected in the liturgical music of African-Americans and the unpublished homilies and theological papers of African-American Catholic preachers and emerging theologians.[10]

African-American Catholic Theology insofar as it is an articulation of the black experience of the Christian faith will necessarily continue the liberation motif of all Black Theology. Where it will differ will probably be in the theological presuppositions and sources which still distinguish Protestant and Catholic thought and in its intentional dialogical engagement with the dogmatic and doctrinal traditions of the Catholic Church.

The Theological Phases and Methodology of Black Catholic Theology
African-American Catholic Theology, like black and feminist theology is developing by engaging in the three major tasks of any liberation theology; critique, retrieval and construction.[11] Furthermore the stages are occurring in the organic and simultaneously Afro-circular pattern of development characteristic of Black cultures. Black Catholic liturgical practitioners and musicians found the liturgical expression within Black Catholic Churches to be bland and spiritually deadening. They began to experiment with music, readings, symbols and gestures which more properly reflected the genius and spirit of African Americans and which would nurture their understanding of the challenge of the gospel and the awareness of the indwelling Spirit working within them. They re-examined the theology of Catholic worship and they began publishing their insights and experimentation. These developments were repeated independently across the country and were eventually transmitted by through liturgical con-

ferences sponsored by the National Office of Black Catholics. The NOBC publications reported the research and experiments of these practitioners and most notably of our first African American liturgical scholar, Clarence Joseph Rivers. Most recently these efforts bore fruit in the form of the publication of the African American hymnal, *Lead Me Guide Me*[12] and in an articulation of Black Catholic reflections on cultural adaptations which are "authentically black and truly Catholic" entitled *In Spirit and Truth: Reflection on the Order of the Mass, written* by Jay Glenn Murray and promulgated by the Black Liturgy Subcommittee of the National Council of Catholic Bishops' Committee on the Liturgy.[13]

African-American critical theology will also want to be in dialogue with the contemporary theologies arising and within the Catholic and Protestant communities of other oppressed groups of Black Hispanics, Asian and Natives People in the United States and similar groups in Africa, Latin America and Asia. Feminist liberation theologies throughout the world and theologies arising from the dominant culture theology of European and Euro-American males will also be important dialogue partners. African American Catholic theology will affirm and concur with the insights arise from these various groups while raising critical question regarding other insights and understandings insofar as the latter do not consider the negative impact of their some of their thinking on the social and ecclesial experience of African Americans. In this polycentric intercultural theological dialogue the focus should center on preparing the Catholic Community, nation and world for a level of spiritual and moral action which is preparatory for the realization of the Kingdom in our global village.

The task of retrieval will take scholarly researchers into the archives of the Vatican, the archives of Office for the Propagation of the Faith , dioceses, Catholic parishes in the South and North who had African American parishioners, the archives of the Josephites, the Oblate Sisters of Providence, the Sisters of the Holy Family, the Sisters of the Blessed Sacrament, the Society of the Divine Word, The Holy Ghost Fathers (Spiritans) and other religious congregations of men and women who participated in the early Catholic mission in Black America. In addition the researcher will want to peruse civic and Catholic newspaper, the pages of history, social scion, old and contemporary black poetry and the oral testimony of past and contemporary Black Catholics to surface the African American Contributions and theological understandings about God, Christ, Mission, Salvation, Humanity etc. The historical search has in some instances been initiated from questions that have arisen in the context of pastoral practice. Individuals and groups both amateur and professional are gathering the basic data.[14]

Theology: A Portrait in Black represented the first formal attempt of constructive Black-Catholic Theology. The writings evidence considerable reflection from the depths of the black experience, " at times intuitive, at times systematic, always holistic."[15] Formally credentialed theologians from the African American Catholic community are now emerging on the theological horizon. Several of the original conference participants pursued advance graduate and doctoral studies in theology and pastorally related disciplines and are gradually beginning to publish articles in which they are expressing in original and more theologically sophisticated manner a Black Catholic theological perspectives. The ten year interim (1978-1988) has allowed these emerging theologians time to begin their scholarly research and to think more deeply about the particular characteristics of African American life from a cultural, psychological and historical perspective and to probe more extensively the traditional theological sources and the writings of our classical Catholic and contemporary Catholic and Protestant theologians.

The task begun at the First symposium is being continued by the Degree and Certificate faculties of the Institute for Black Catholic Studies located at Xavier University in New Orleans, Louisiana. Those who specialize in theology will continue in dialogue with shoe from the disciplines of philosophy, anthropology, history, psychology, economics, literature and the arts and any field of study which deepens the understand of our particular cultural group under the broad umbrella of peoples of African descent and the more specific umbrella of African American or African American Catholics, Given this reality, this theology will most like be forged by a community of theologians in dialogue[16] with ecclesial comminutes of African American Catholics, Africa American bishops, pastors and preachers, participants in the Institute for Black Catholic Studies, as well as within interdisciplinary symposia similar to the original gathering in 1978, The dialogue is open to expansion by interaction with the other cultural communities of critical theology mentioned above.

The criteria of truth of this African American Catholic Theology will perhaps be threefold beginning with a sense of the meaning and interpretation of the reality and desire for the authentic human condition of African Americans created by God the creator and sustained by the Holy Spirit (orthopathy or "sensum fidelium");[17] a coherent theoretical search for truth consistent with a critical reading of the diverse traditions with Catholic Tradition (orthodoxy) and finally an authentic emergence of life engendering thought and action which can transform unjust and evil realities into a just and loving realities (orthopraxy). This theological enterprise of faith seeking understanding within the context of the Black life experience will ask three primary and interrelated questions. Are those theological interpretations which already exist or which are emerging continuous or discontinuous with that which has been taught and believed within the dogmatic and doctrinal traditions of Catholicism? Are these theological interpretation of the tradition and contemporary theology giving rise to action on behalf of justice which transform society and the church? And finally do these theological interpretations give rise to a passionate fife-giving appropriation of the gospel which bears the fruit of spiritual and social transformation of the African American community in general and the African American Catholic community in particular. All three criteria will be subordinated to the prime questions of life transformation evidenced by the life energy which characterizes a community which has assumed its own proper dignity and responsibility as subjects acting in history empowered by the Holy Spirit. Does the theological formulations help the African American community in general and the African American Catholic community in particular recognize the abundance of life which Jesus promised to all God's disciples? (I have come that you may have life and live k to the frill (John 10:10)) African American Catholic frilly alive will be empowered by the Holy Spirit with the spiritual energy to challenge the American Community and the world church and community to transform itself into and all-inclusive worldwide communion of justice, peace and love!

The task is enormous, the laborers are few. Let us pray for an increasing harvest of theologians dedicated to this ministry. May the Spirit who began God's work in us, bring it to completion?

Conclusion

The two million plus members of the African-American Catholic Community in the United States is a culturally, economically psychologically complex community whose individual and collective experience forms the basic community from which Black-Catholic theology arises. The historical and paradigmatic events which shaped the Black community within the United States into an identifiable community was Slavery and the Civil War and their aftermath. All visible Blacks share in the common oppression of institutional racism and its accompanying abuses which were inaugurated by these events. That which shapes Black Catholics also include is the history of Black peoples sojourn within the Catholic Communities of the "New World."

The sources of Black-Catholic Theology will accordingly start with the historical and contemporary individual and collective experience of African-Americans and African-American dialogue with Catholic dogmatic traditions. Catholics interpreted by and interpreting the Scriptural, and the Dogmatic traditions of Roman Catholicism. African-American Catholic Theology insofar as it is an articulation of the black experience of the Christian faith shares common ground with Black theology. It may diverge in areas of the theological assumptions which still divide the Protestant and Catholic communities and Black-Catholic Theologies.

Currently, the phases of liberation theology are phases of Black-Catholic Theology as evidenced by the processes of Black-Catholic liturgical development and the stages of critique, retrieval and constructive theology evident at the Black Catholic Theological Symposium of 1978 The methodological context will include interdisciplinary, pastoral and collective dialogue. The criteria of truth which are emerging are threefold: the theology must be dogmatically correct, it must inspire the ethical behavior required by justice and be rooted in the Spirit whose presence is evidenced by an emotional and passionate appropriation of the biblical commitment to love, peace and justice which bear fruit in the transformation of the community.[4]

Notes

[1] This previously unpublished paper was first presented at the Catholic Theological Society of America (CTSA) in June of 1988 in Toronto Canada and was circulated privately among several of the Black Catholic theo-

logical scholars. It is referred to in Dr. Copeland's article "Foundations for Catholic Theology in an African American Context" p. 139. Some slight changes were made for accuracy but the edited article (particularly the footnotes) maintained the historical horizon of the African American Catholic Community and Theological development in 1988.

[2] Alice Walker, *In Search of our Mothers' Gardens*. (New York: Harcourt Brace Jovanovich, 1983), 49.

[3] The social-economic conditions of African-Americans is reviewed annually in a research report issued by the National Urban League, Inc. which was founded in 1910. See the *State of Black America* ed. Janet Deawart (New York; National Urban League, 1988) Basic Statistics about the African Americans. The social-economic conditions of African-Americans is reviewed annually in a research report issued by the National Urban League, Inc. which was founded in 1910. Basic Statistics about African American Catholics are available from the Josephite Pastoral Center and the Secretariat for Black Catholics of the United States Catholic Conference both located in Washington, D.C. Diocesan information is available from the Offices of Black Catholics or Ethnic Ministries in each diocese where they have been established. The Divine Word Publication "In a Word" based in Bay St. Louis, Mississippi and the *National Catholic Mentor* newspaper published in Memphis, Tennessee are regularly published organs and sources of Black Catholic reflections and issues.

[4] This African American categories or types were created on the basis of the authors participant observation as a member of several parish staffs in the Archdiocese of Chicago and in her work as a national consultant for Black Catholic Ministry. Thaddeus Posey, O.F.M., Cap., noted in a conversation that the third type is described in a study of Martin Luther King Jr., by Kenneth Smith and Ira G. Zipp, Jr., in *Searching for the Beloved Community* (Valley Forge: Judson Press, 1974). This desire to be recognized as American without losing one's distinct African American cultural identity was termed "black consciousness" in W.E.B. Dubois class work, *The Souls of Black Folk* originally published in 1910.

[5] Participants in this original symposium included M. Shawn Copeland, Jamie T. Phelps, O.P., and Rev. Thaddeus Posey, O.F.M. Cap., are Ph.D. candidates in Theology. Shawn and Jamie have teaching positions at Yale, and the Catholic Theological Union, respectfully. Thaddeus is the director of the Summer Black-Catholic Institute at Xavier University, New Orleans. John Ford is pursuing a doctorate in pastoral counseling. Dr. Toinette Eugene completed a doctorate in the Sociology of Religion and is currently Provost of the Divinity School of Colgate-Rochester. Dr. Giles Conwill completed a doctorate in Anthropology and is teaching in Atlanta. Fr. Joseph Perry completed a Canon Law degree and works in the Milwaukee Wisconsin Chancery office. Rev. Jerome Le Doux, S.V.D., J. C.D., had completed his canon law degree. Reverends Edward K. Braxton, Paul GoPaul, S.S.E., and Joseph Nearon, S.S.S.,

already had doctorates in Theology, while Rev. Cyprian Davis, O.S.B., Sr. Thea Bowman, F.S.P.A., Rev. Clarence Rivers, Brother Cyprian Rowe, F.M.S., already had doctorates in Church History, Literature, Liturgy and African Studies, respectively. Rev. Bede Abrams, O.F.M. Conv., had completed his licentiate in theology and teaches at Xavier University, New Orleans. Other participants have been honing their pastoral skills in various areas of expertise: Rev. Albert McKnight, C.S.Sp., and Rev. August Thompson (Community Economic Development and pastoral action), George Stalls (Preaching and Evangelization), Glenn Jean-Marie and Ferdnand Cheri (Liturgy). Three participants have been elevated to the Episcopacy: Most Reverends James P. Lyke, O.F.M., Terry Steib, S.V.D., and Moses Anderson, S.S.E.

This original interdisciplinary brain and "soul" trust has been augmented by other African-American Catholics. Ms. Diana Hayes is Ph.D. candidate in Theology. Sr. Delores Harrall, S.N.D. (Ph.D. in Education), Dr. Nathan Jones (Religious Education), Rev. Leonard Scott, J.C.D., Sr. Francesca Thompson, O.S.F. (Ph.D. in Literature and Drama), Rev. Hugh Stout, Ph.D. (Sociology), Sr. Addie Walker, S.S.N.D., ThM and Eva Marie Lumas, S.S.S., Th.M. (master cathechists), Sr. Constance Phelps, S.C.L. (Ph.D. in Sociology), Dr. Audrey Campbell, Rev. Charles Payne, O.F.M., Ph.D., Dr. Edwin Nichols (all in the field of Psychology), Rev. Joseph Brown, S.J., Ph.D., who has a Ph.D. in American Studies with specialization in African American Literature from Yale.

[6] Joseph Nearon, "Introduction," ed. by Thaddeus Posey, O.F.M. Cap., *Theology :A Portrait in Black,* Proceedings of the 1978 Black Catholic Theological Symposium (Washington, D.C. : National Black Catholic Clergy Caucus, 1980). Private Circulation available through the Institute for Black Catholic Studies, Xavier University, New Orleans.

[7] M. Shawn Copeland has a more detailed and critical chapter forthcoming entitled "African- American Catholics and Black Theology: An Interpretation" ed. By Gayraud Wilmore *Afro-American Religious Studies: An Interdisciplinary Approach* (Durham: Duke University Press, 1989). In the article she gives an overview of the Black Catholic Movement that began in 1968 with the founding of the National Black Catholic Clergy Caucus (NBCCC), the National Black Sisters Conference (NBSC), the National Office of Black Catholics (NOBC) and the National Black Seminarians Association (NBSA).

[8] Albert Raboteau, *Slave Religion.* (New York: Oxford University Press, 1980). C. Eric Lincoln, *Religion and the Continuing American Dilemma* New York: Hill and Wang, 1984). Gayraud, S. Wilmore, *Black Religion and Black Radicalism* (New York: Orbis Press, 1983).

[9] See such sociology of religion and psychological sources as Leonard E. Barrett, *Soul Force* (New York: Anchor Press/Doubleday, 1974) and Alfred B. Pasteur, and Ivory L. Toldson, *Roots of Soul* (New York: Anchor Press/Doubleday, 1982)

[10] *Lead Me, Guide Me: The African-American Catholic Hymnal.* (Chicago: G.I.A. Publications, 1987.)

[11] This three-stage schema is described by Jacquelyn Grant, Ph.D., as the three tasks of liberation theology. See her "A Black Response to Feminist Theology," *Women's Spirit Bonding,* ed. By Janet Kalven and Mary I. Buckley (New York: Pilgrim Press, 1984), 117-24.

[12] Op. cit. The hymnal Committee included Bishops James P. Lyke, O.F.M.; Wilton D. Gregory, Rev. Arthur Anderson, O.F.M.; Mr. Edmund C. Broussard; Mrs. Marjorie Gabriel-Burros; Mr. Avon Gillespie; Mr. Rawn Harbor; Sister Laura Marie Kendricks, H.V.M.; Mr. Leon Roberts; Mr. Ronald Sharps; and Brother Bob Smith, O.F.M., Cap.

[13] *In Spirit and Truth: Black Catholic Reflections on the Order of the Mass* (USCC, Washington, D.C., 1988). This subcommittee was chaired by Most Rev. Wilton D. Gregory, auxiliary Bishop of Chicago who previously taught liturgy on the faculty of St. Mary's Seminary, Mundelein. Two other bishops, Archbishop Lipscomb of Mobile and James P. Lyke, O.F.M., were joined by Black priests, deacons and laymen and women who were actively engaged in liturgical ministry in the Black-Catholic parishes; Mrs. Margaret Guillery Armendez, Rev. Ferdnand J. Cheri, Mr. Norah Duncan, Ms. Carole V. Norris, Rev. William Norvel, Sr. Mary Roger Thibodeaux, S.B.S., and Deacon Marvin Threatt. This reflection was preceded by writings on Black-Catholic Liturgy by numerous African-American liturgical practitioners and some liturgists. The most notable liturgical scholar is Rev. Clarence Joseph Rivers, who was a prime mover in the liturgical renewal in the United States as well as in the Black-Catholic Community. His creative genius is recorded in his music and publications: *Celebrations* (New York: Herder & Herder, 1969) and *Reflections* (New York: Herder & Herder, 1970); *Soulful Worship* (Washington, D.C: National Office of Black Catholics, 1974); This *Far by Faith* (Washington, D.C.: National Office of Black Catholics); *The Spirit in Worship* (Cincinnati: Stimuli Inc., 1978) and selections in *Freeing the Spirit* (Washington, D.C.: National Office of Black Catholics) Vol 1–Vol 6 (1971-1974).

[14] Unfortunately these sources of retrieval have been generally ignored or have been treated sparsely by in American Catholic History texts. However, has issued several volumes focused on the Black Catholic historical experience, to date have appeared under the editorship of Christopher J. Kauffman, "The Black Catholic Experience" *U.S. Catholic Historian* vol 5 no. 1 (1986) and "The Black Catholic Community, 1880-1987" *U.S. Catholic Historian* vol. 7, nos. 2 and 3 (Spring/Summer, 1988). Cyprian Davis, O.S.B., is currently working on The History of Black Catholics in the United States (New York: Crossroads, publication pending). Marilyn Nickels is working on a manuscript entitled *Black Catholic Protest and the Federated Colored Catholics, 1917-1933* (New York: Garland, publication pending). The work focuses on a lay Black Catholic organization found in the early twentieth century. Stephen Ochs of the Uni-

versity of Maryland is working on a manuscript from his extensive dissertation which focused on the struggle for the development of an African American Catholic clergy within the United States entitled *Desegregating the Altar: the Josephites and the Struggle for Black Priests 1871-1960* (Baton Rouge, Louisiana State University Press, publication pending). Jamie Phelps is completing a dissertation which focuses on the theological and historical foundation for the African American Catholic mission in the United States entitled *The Mission Ecclesiology of John R. Slattery*, Wm. L. Portier of St. Mary's Emmitsburgh, is working on a biography of Slattery with emphasis on his Americanist and Modernist connections. Randall M. Miller and Jon L. Wakelyn's *Catholics in the Old South* (Atlanta: Mercer University Press, 1983) also provides some data for the retrieval. Private group have support the efforts of amateur and professional historians writing brief local histories of Black Catholics e.g., Nathaniel Green, *The Silent Believers* (Louisville: West End Catholic Council, 1972); Madeline B. Oliver and William B. Flaherty, S.J., *The Religious Roots of Black Catholics of St. Louis* (St. Louis: St. Stanislaus Historic Museum, Inc., 1877). A Black Catholic History Project has been commissioned by the office of Black Catholic Ministries of the Washington Archdiocese.

[15] Thaddeus Posey, "Preface," *Theology: A Portrait in Black*, 4. Rev. Thaddeus Posey, O.F.M. Cap., convened the first Black Catholic Theological Symposium and is the Founding Director of the Institute for Black Catholics Studies of Xavier University in New Orleans. He inaugurated these initiatives as projects of the National Black Catholic Clergy Caucus in consultation with many other people notable among his initial planning consultants were Fathers August Taylor and David Benz, Joseph Nearon and Sr. Jamie T. Phelps, O.P.

[16] I am grateful for the listening and critical ear of Dr. Toinette Eugene, M. Shawn Copeland and Father Thaddeus Posey, O.F.M. Cap., for supplying some specific date for this article and to Fr. Steve Bevans, S.V.D., for his listening ear and critical eye in reviewing the draft of this text..

[17] The writer first heard the term "orthopathy" in a lecture given by Toinette Eugene. In the context she was referring to emotional feeling and passion that is characteristic of African-American life and is found in the biblical tradition particularly in the prophetic traditions of Amos and Hosea as well as in the Marcan Gospel. It is this emotional, feeling and passionate aspect of African-American faith which gives rise to the search for authentic doctrine (orthodoxy) and authentic action (orthopraxis).

[18] Throughout these footnotes and I have identified the titles , degrees and contributions of a number of African American Catholic done to continue the African tradition of celebrating and honoring those whose individual gifts have been developed and exercised for the benefit of the community. Many names not listed here have already been lost to recorded history but God does not forget.

About the Contributors

Diane Bergant, C.S.A. Ph.D., is Professor of Old Testament Studies at the Catholic Theological Union in Chicago, Illinois, and the second Director of D. Min. Program sponsored jointly by Catholic Theological Union, Lutheran School of Theology, and McCormick Theological Seminary in Chicago, Illinois. She completed her B.S. in Elementary Education at Marian College in Fond du Lac, Wisconsin, in 1961. She received her M.A. and Ph.D. in Biblical Languages and Literature from Saint Louis University, St. Louis. Missouri, in 1970 and 1975 respectively.

M. Shawn Copeland, Ph.D., is Associate Professor of Theology at Marquette University in Milwaukee, Wisconsin, and a member of the summer degree faculty of the Institute for Black Catholic Studies of Xavier University in New Orleans, Louisiana. She completed her B.A. in English Literature in 1969 at Madonna College in Livonia, Michigan. She received her Ph.D. in Systematic Theology from Boston College, Boston, Massachusetts, in 1991.

Cyprian Davis, OSB, D. Hist, Sc., is Professor of Church History and Archivist at Saint Meinrad School of Theology and Monastery. He is also a founding member of the summer degree faculty of the Institute for Black Catholic Studies of Xavier University in New Orleans, Louisiana. He completed an S.T.L, at The Catholic University of American in Washington, D.C., in 1957. He received his L.Hist. Sc. and D.Hist.Sc. from the Catholic University of Louvain (Belgium) in 1963 and 1977 respectively.

Bryan Massingale, S.T.D., is Associate Professor of Moral Theology at St. Francis Seminary in Milwaukee, Wisconsin, and a member of the summer degree faculty of the Institute for Black Catholic Studies of Xavier University, in New Orleans. He completed his B.A. in Theology, Philosophy, and Psychology at Marquette University in 1979. He received his S.T.L. in Moral Theology from the Catholic University of America, Washington, D.C., in 1988 and his S.T.D., also in Moral Theology, from the Academia Alphonsianum, Rome, Italy, in 1991.

Jamie T. Phelps, O.P. Ph.D., is Associate Professor of Doctrinal and Mission Theology at Catholic Theological Union in Chicago, Illinois, and the Associate Director and faculty member for the Degree Program at the Institute for Black Catholic Studies of Xavier University in New Orleans. She was the founding Director of the Augustus Tolton Pastoral Ministry program, a graduate degree program for educating African American lay women and men for professional ministry in the Chicago Archdiocese (1988-1996). She completed her B.A. in Sociology at Siena Heights College, Adrian, Michigan, in 1969. She received her M.S.W. (Masters in Social Work) from the University of Illinois at Chicago in 1972, her M.A. in Scripture and Systematic Theology from St. John's University in Collegeville, Minnesota, in 1975, and her Ph.D. in Systematic Theology from The Catholic University of America, Washington, D.C., in 1989.

Paul Wadell, C.P. Ph.D., is Professor of Ethics at Catholic Theological Union in Chicago. He completed his B. A. in English at Bellarmine College in Louisville, Kentucky, in 1973. He received his M.Div. (Master of Divinity) and his M.A. in Moral Theology from the Catholic Theological Union, Chicago, Illinois, in 1978 and 1980 respectively, and his Ph.D. in Christian Ethics from Notre Dame University, Notre Dame, Indiana, in 1985.

Vincent L. Wimbush, Ph.D., is Professor of New Testament and Christian Origins at Union Theological Seminary in New York City. He completed his B.A. in Philosophy at Morehouse College in 1975. He received his M.Div. from Yale University in 1978, and his M.A. and Ph.D., in the Study of Religion: New Testament and Christian Origins, from Harvard University Graduate School of Arts and Sciences in 1981 and 1983 respectively.

Martin Zielinski, Ph.D., is Associate Professor of Church History and served as Academic Dean of Mundelein Seminary of the University of St. Mary of the Lake, Mundelein, Illinois, 1991–1997. He completed his B.A. in Communication Arts at Loyola University in Chicago, Illinois, in 1974. He received his M.Div. from Mundelein Seminary in 1978, and his M.A. and Ph.D. in Church History from the Catholic University of America in Washington, D.C., in 1985 and 1989 respectively.

Index